Controlling Silica Exposures in Construction

I0473946

Occupational Safety and Health Administration
U.S. Department of Labor

OSHA 3362-04
2009

Cover photo courtesy of the Center to Protect Workers' Rights (CPWR)

Contents

Overview

This guidance document addresses the control of employee exposures to respirable dust containing crystalline silica, which is known to cause silicosis, a serious lung disease, as well as increase the risk of lung cancer and other systemic diseases. This document provides information on the effectiveness of various engineering control approaches for several kinds of construction operations and equipment, and contains recommendations for work practices and respiratory protection, as appropriate.

Quartz is the most common form of crystalline silica. In fact, it is the second most common surface material accounting for almost 12% by volume of the earth's crust. Quartz is present in many materials in the construction industry, such as brick and mortar, concrete, slate, dimensional stone (granite, sandstone), stone aggregate, tile, and sand used for blasting. Other construction materials that contain crystalline silica are asphalt filler, roofing granules, plastic composites, soils, and to a lesser extent, some wallboard joint compounds, paint, plaster, caulking and putty. Cristobalite, a less common form of crystalline silica, is formed at high temperatures (>1,470°C) in nature and by industrial processes. The ceramic and brick lining of boilers and vessels, some ceramic tiles, and volcanic ash contain cristobalite.

The crystalline silica permissible exposure limit (PEL) for the construction industry at 29 CFR 1926.55(a) is expressed in terms of millions of particles per cubic foot (mppcf). This PEL is based on a particle count method long rendered obsolete by respirable mass (gravimetric) sampling, which yields results reported in milligrams per cubic meter (mg/m^3). In contrast with the construction PEL, the crystalline silica PEL for general industry is based on gravimetric sampling, which is the only method currently available to OSHA compliance personnel. Since the construction PEL is expressed in terms of mppcf, the results of the gravimetric sampling must be converted to an equivalent mppcf value. For more information on the conversion of gravimetric sampling results, please see Appendix E of OSHA Directive CPL 03-00-007 (January 24, 2008). It can be accessed at http://www.osha.gov/pls/oshaweb/owadisp.show_document?p_ table=DIRECTIVES& p_id=3790.

In this guidance, OSHA uses a benchmark 8-hour time-weighted average exposure of 0.1 mg/m^3 of respirable silica dust as a point of reference in describing control measures utilized by the construction trades. This benchmark is more conserva-tive (i.e., lower) than the current construction PEL. The benchmark is approximately equivalent to the general industry PEL, is a single easy-to-use number rather than a formula, and is expressed in terms of the current gravimetric method rather than the obsolete particle count method. Since this benchmark is generally more conservative than the construction PEL, employers who meet the benchmark will be in compliance with the construction PEL. OSHA notes that some organizations have recommended lower levels. For example, the National Institute for Occupational Safety and Health (NIOSH) recommends that respirable crystalline silica exposures be limited to 0.05 mg/m^3 as a time-weighted average for up to 10 hours (NIOSH, 2002). The American Conference of Government Industrial Hygienists (ACGIH) recommends that respirable crystalline silica exposures be limited to 0.025 as an 8-hour time-weighted average (ACGIH, 2008). OSHA is reviewing the construction and general industry PELs for silica in its ongoing silica rulemaking.

The recommendations presented in this document are based on a review of information in the published literature, NIOSH In-Depth Survey Reports and OSHA inspection data. Engineering control evaluations reported in the published literature were generally performed in controlled work environments and may not reflect actual workplace exposures experienced at construction worksites. Moreover, potential silica exposure levels will depend on the concentration of silica in materials at construction sites, as well as factors in the work environment (such as enclosed, semi-enclosed, or open spaces and/or multiple operations generating silica dust) as well as environmental conditions (such as wind direction and speed). Therefore, OSHA encourages employers to conduct periodic exposure monitoring to confirm that engineering and work practice controls are effective and that appropriate respiratory protection is being used where necessary. Controls continue to evolve and OSHA encourages equipment suppliers and contractors to work with industrial hygienists to evaluate new designs and products to obtain objective information that can be used to evaluate performance and support informed decisions on use.

If you choose to modify equipment, it is important to follow equipment manufacturers' recommendations in order to ensure that modifications do not adversely affect equipment performance and that no additional hazards are created. Furthermore, ground-fault circuit interrupters (GFCI) and watertight/sealable electrical connectors should be used with electric tools and equipment on construction sites (OSHA, 1996). These features are particularly important in areas where water is used to control dust.

The document is divided into nine sections that cover different construction operations. Eight are for specific equipment or operations: Stationary Masonry Saws, Handheld Masonry Saws, Hand-Operated Grinders, Tuckpointing/Mortar Removal, Jackhammers, Rotary Hammers and Similar Tools, Vehicle-Mounted Rock Drilling Rigs, and Drywall Finishing. The other section addresses general housekeeping operations and dust control through the use of dust suppressants. These nine sections draw heavily from OSHA's experience, as is reflected in the numerous references to "OSHA case files." These files originated primarily from OSHA's Region 5 in conjunction with a Special Emphasis Program for silica, and can be found in a report prepared for OSHA by Eastern Research Group (ERG). This report, "Technological Feasibility Study and Cost Impact Analysis of the Draft Crystalline Silica Standard for Construction", can be found in draft form in OSHA's docket H-006A, and at http://dockets.osha.gov/vg001/V037B/00/01/28.PDF.

The sections have been carefully written and compiled; they include case studies, reference lists, and technical notes. They offer information, advice and recommendations on using wet methods, vacuum dust collection (VDC) systems, and work practices to control dust emissions from construction operations. Many of these dust control systems are readily available from vendors. By implementing these recommendations, employers will more effectively minimize employee exposures to respirable dust containing crystalline silica and will provide a safer work environment for their employees.

For additional information about controlling silica exposures in construction, please see OSHA's website at http://www.osha.gov/SLTC/construction silica/index.html.

Stationary Masonry Saws

This section covers gas- and electric-powered stationary masonry saws. The term "silica" used in this document refers to respirable crystalline silica.

Introduction

Exposure to fine particles of silica has been shown to cause silicosis, a serious and sometimes fatal lung disease. Construction employees who inhale fine particles of silica may be at risk of developing this disease. Employees produce dusts containing silica when they cut, grind, crush, or drill construction materials such as concrete, masonry, tile and rock. The small particles easily become suspended in the air and, when inhaled, penetrate deep into employees' lungs.

Studies show that using a stationary masonry saw to cut bricks, concrete blocks and similar materials can result in hazardous levels of airborne silica if measures are not taken to reduce dust emissions. Stationary saws should always be used with dust control measures. At worksites without dust controls for these tools, studies have found that employee silica exposures can be as high as 20 times the Occupational Safety and Health Administration's (OSHA) benchmark of 0.1 mg/m³ (milligrams per cubic meter of air) as an 8-hour time-weighted average (TWA), an exposure approximately equivalent to OSHA's general industry permissible exposure limit (PEL) (OSHA Case Files).[1] Short-term exposures can be even higher.

This section describes methods available to reduce employees' exposures to silica when using stationary masonry saws. OSHA encourages you to use this information to evaluate or improve system performance to reduce dust emissions. Technical notes are found at the end of this section and are referenced throughout the text.

Hazardous exposures to silica can occur when stationary saws are operated without appropriate dust controls. (Photo courtesy of the University of Washington.)

Two primary methods exist to control silica dust while operating a stationary saw: (1) wet cutting, and (2) vacuum dust collection. Ventilated booths, when properly designed, can also reduce silica dust exposure. All of these methods are easy to implement.

Wet cutting, when used properly, is an effective way to reduce employee exposures to silica dust and in most cases maintains exposures below the allowable limit. *Vacuum dust collection* can significantly reduce silica levels, but may not reliably keep them below 0.1 mg/m³ as an 8-hour TWA.

Silica Dust Control Measures

Wet Cutting

Most stationary saws come equipped with a water basin that typically holds several gallons of water and a pump for recycling water for wet cutting.[2] If a saw's water supply system is not currently operating, the manufacturer may be able to supply the necessary accessories to reactivate wet cutting capability. Most suppliers stock these accessories since water cooling prolongs the life of the saw blade and tool.

Wet cutting is the most effective method for controlling silica dust generated during sawing because it controls the exposure at its source. Dust that is wet is less able to become or remain airborne. Results obtained by OSHA and the National Institute for Occupational Safety and Health (NIOSH) at five construction sites indicate that wet masonry saw operators' exposures were routinely below 0.1 mg/m3, and usually below 0.05 mg/m³, not only when averaged over an 8-hour shift, but also during just the period evaluated.[3]

At one jobsite, for example, NIOSH recorded a respirable silica exposure level of 0.04 mg/m³ in the breathing zone of an employee cutting concrete blocks using a water-fed bench saw. The employee operated the saw for approximately 5 of the 8 hours sampled (NIOSH, 1999a). Even if the employee had cut block for a full 8-hour shift, his estimated exposure would have been 0.05 mg/m³.

In comparison, OSHA reported a significantly higher exposure at another site on a day when wet methods were not used due to cold weather. The employee dry cut concrete block outdoors for a similar period of time (nearly 6 hours), but in this case experienced an 8-hour average exposure of 2 mg/m³ (OSHA Case Files).[4]

Employee exposures associated with uncontrolled dry cutting tend to be lower for employees operating saws for a smaller percentage of their shift, as well as for jobs involving materials with lower silica content. However, among the nine results obtained by OSHA and NIOSH, the average exposure for dry cutting outdoors was 0.56 mg/m³ (with a median of 0.25 mg/m³) for the periods sampled.[5] These values exceed OSHA limits, and were associated with employees dry cutting for 10 to 60 percent of the time sampled. At three construction sites, employee exposures exceeded 2 mg/m³, presumably during periods of intensive cutting lasting from 2 minutes to 6 hours (Lofgren, 1993; OSHA Case Files).

Maintenance. To minimize dust emissions from saws equipped for wet cutting, keep pumps, hoses and nozzles in excellent operating condition. Regular saw maintenance reduces silica exposures and ensures optimal operation of the equipment. Saws and dust control devices should be on a routine maintenance schedule.

Maintaining a Water-Feed System

- Check the pump to ensure that it is working properly and make sure that hoses are securely connected and not cracked or broken.
- Adjust nozzles to ensure that water is directed so that the maximum amount reaches the cutting area while still cooling the blade.
- Rinse or replace water filters at appropriate intervals to ensure that the flow of clean water is not restricted and to prevent damage to the pump.
- Replace basin water when it gets gritty or begins to silt up with dust. Depending on use, this step may need to be repeated several times per day to prevent the nozzle from clogging and to ensure that mist generated during cutting does not carry extra dust from the recycled water.
- Dispose of water containing silica in a way that prevents the silica from becoming resuspended in the air. If the silica is allowed to become airborne, it can contribute to employee exposures.
- Consult the manufacturer for equipment operating specifications and recommendations that apply to the specific saw model including electrical fault protection, such as a ground-fault circuit interrupter (GFCI).

Freezing Temperatures. Freezing temperatures complicate the use of water.[6] Consider heating the local work area, if practical, to prevent ice from forming in the water-feed system. Drain the system when not in use. Large portable heating units are commonly used to heat commercial and sometimes road and highway projects. If water freezes on the ground, chip away the ice or use deicing compounds or sand to control the slipping hazard.

Electrical Safety. Use ground-fault circuit interrupters (GFCIs) and watertight, sealable electrical connectors for electric tools and equipment on construction sites (OSHA, 1996). These features are particularly important to employee safety in wet or damp areas, such as where water is used to control dust. Although an assured equipment grounding conductor program is an acceptable alternative to GFCIs, OSHA recommends that employers use GFCIs where possible because they afford better protection for employees. (See 29 CFR 1926.404(b)(1) for OSHA's ground-fault protection requirements.)

Visible and Respirable Dust

Visible dust contains large particles that are easy to see. The tiny, respirable-sized particles (those that can get into the deep lung) containing silica pose the greatest hazard and are not visible. Most dust-generating construction activities produce a mixture of visible and respirable particles.

Do use visible dust as a general guide for improving dust suppression efforts. If you see visible dust being generated, emissions of respirable silica are probably too high. Measures that control tool-generated dust at the source usually reduce all types of particle emissions, including respirable particles.

Do not rely only on visible dust to assess the extent of the silica hazard. There may be more airborne respirable dust present that is not visible to the naked eye.

Vacuum Dust Collection Systems

When wet methods cannot be implemented, one alternative is the use of vacuum dust collection (VDC) systems. Stationary masonry saws with VDC systems are commercially available and have the ability to capture a substantial amount of dust.

With these systems, a vacuum pulls dust from the cutting point through special fittings connected directly to the saw (fixed-blade saws) or, alternatively, through a dust collection device connected to the back of the saw (plunge-cut saws) (Croteau, 2000). A dust collector (exterior hood) mounted to the back of a saw requires a high exhaust airflow to ensure good dust capture between the saw blade and dust collector.

Under experimental conditions, a VDC system for a fixed-blade saw reduced short-term (15-minute) exposures by 80 to 95 percent when compared to uncontrolled masonry cutting. Because the saw produced unusually high levels of dust in the enclosed, ventilated test area, the operators' silica exposure levels exceeded OSHA limits by a wide margin, even with the VDC system equipment activated. However, the authors of the study reported that uncontrolled silica exposure levels in the study were considerably greater than those observed in actual construction industry exposure assessment studies. Consequently, use of the VDC system in an actual construction setting could reduce silica exposure levels below OSHA limits (Croteau, 2000; Croteau et al., 2002). Even when operators' silica exposure still exceeds OSHA limits, the level of exposure could be substantially reduced through the use of the VDC system.

Recommendations for Vacuum Dust Collection Systems. The American Conference of Governmental Industrial Hygienists (ACGIH) recommends airflow of 25 cubic feet per minute (CFM) per inch of blade diameter (ACGIH, 2007). If airflow is too low, the hose may clog with particulate matter. A study by Croteau et al. (2002), which tested an abrasive wheel saw, indicated that a ventilation flow rate of 75 CFM and an air velocity of 3440 feet per minute (FPM) should be considered the minimum ventilation rate for a 2-inch diameter vacuum hose. If the system provides a higher flow rate, then it is acceptable to use a larger hose.

VDC systems can be purchased as a kit. These kits should include a dust collector (exterior hood), vacuum, vacuum hose, and filter(s). The components of a VDC system are discussed below.

- *Dust collector (exterior hood)*: Be sure to use the appropriate sized dust collector for the wheel and if it is a retrofit on the saw, be sure to follow the manufacturer's instructions when installing the device.

- *Vacuum*: Choose a vacuum with the appropriate power and capacity for your job. Obtaining a flow rate on a VDC system of 80 CFM or better will give the best results while performing mortar removal (Heitbrink and Watkins, 2001).

- *Vacuum hose*: A flow rate of 80 CFM is best maintained with a 1½- to 2-inch diameter hose. If the diameter is larger, the airflow velocity will be reduced. If the diameter is smaller, airflow resistance will be higher. Airflow resistance also increases with hose length; excessively long hoses should be avoided.

- *Filters*: Double filtration is important. The use of a high-efficiency particulate air (HEPA) filter is critical to prevent the escape of respirable silica dust from the vacuum exhaust. HEPA filters are at least 99.97 percent efficient in removing fine dust particles from the air. A prefilter or cyclonic separator in addition to a HEPA filter will improve vacuum efficiency and extend the service life of the more costly HEPA filter. A cyclonic separator removes large particles that are capable of overloading or clogging the filter (Heitbrink and Collingwood, 2005).[7]

- *Systematic cleaning*: Choose a vacuum equipped with a back-pulse filter cleaning cycle. Such auto-cleaning mechanisms will reduce the time required for vacuum maintenance and improve the overall efficiency of the dust collection system. If the vacuum does not have an auto-cleaning mechanism, the employee can periodically turn the vacuum cleaner on and off. This allows the bag to collapse and causes the prefilter cake to dislodge from the filter.

- *Monitoring VDC efficiency*: Purchasing a dust collection system equipped with a static pressure gauge allows the employee to monitor the system's efficiency. Systems lacking a static pressure gauge can be monitored visually. If a dust plume increases and becomes more visible where the dust collector meets the working surface, the system is not working efficiently (Heitbrink and Collingwood, 2005).

Tips for Operating a Vacuum Dust Collection System

- Make sure that all hoses are clean and free of cracks.
- Ensure that appropriate filters and dust bags are in good condition and changed or emptied as needed (may be necessary several times per shift under some circumstances).
- Check the entire system daily for signs of poor dust capture or dust leaks.
- Use high-efficiency (HEPA) filters for maximum dust control.
- Erect baffles on either side of the saw to improve dust capture by rear-mounted dust collection devices (exterior hoods).
- Review manufacturers' operating specifications and recommendations for your equipment.

Work Practice Controls to Enhance Vacuum Effectiveness. Studies have shown that the effectiveness of VDC systems is enhanced by the use of proper work practices (NIOSH, 1999; Croteau et al., 2002). However, use of these work techniques without a dust collection system will not substantially reduce dust exposures.

With any type of vacuum system, employee protection from respirable dust is only as good as the filter in the vacuum. The less efficient the filter, the more respirable dust will pass through with the vacuum exhaust air. Locating the vacuum as far from employees as possible is one way to help limit exposure.

For optimal dust collection, the following measures are recommended:

- Keep the vacuum hose clear and free of debris, kinks and tight bends. Maintain the vacuum at peak performance to ensure adequate airflow through the dust collector and vacuum hoses.

- On vacuums with manual back-pulse filter cleaning systems, activate the system frequently (several times per day). Empty collection bags and vacuums as frequently as necessary. Dispose of collected dust in a way that prevents it from becoming resuspended in the air.

- For best results, set up a regular schedule for filter cleaning and maintenance. For example, institute a rule to clean the filter or change the bag at each break. This will prevent pressure loss and ensure that exhaust airflow stays constant on the VDC system.

- Remember, the absence of visible dust does not necessarily mean that employees are adequately protected from silica exposure.

Ventilation Booths

A booth (with fan) erected around a saw can help reduce dust, but may require some experimentation.[8] For example, one employer built a plywood booth around the saw and installed a large exhaust fan at the rear wall to pull dust away from the employee, who operated the saw through an opening in the front of the booth.[9] Initial air sampling results indicated that the operators' exposures to silica while cutting brick were between 0.07 and 0.1 mg/m³. By modifying the booth interior to better capture the plume of dust released by the saw, the employer was able to reduce exposures further, to 0.02 mg/m³ during the period evaluated (OSHA Case Files).[10]

Tips for Designing an Effective Booth[3]
- Minimize the size of the operator opening to reduce the chance of dust escaping into the operator's breathing area.
- Use a fan large enough to provide an average

---

of 250 feet per minute air velocity across the face of the operator opening.
- Do not let the saw blade protrude beyond the open face of the booth.
- Build a trapdoor into the lower back of the booth to access the interior for cleaning and to remove debris.
- Always position the booth so that the exhaust fan does not blow dusty air on other employees. When possible, have the booth exhaust downwind.

Fans

Fans are not effective dust control devices when used as the sole control method and should not be used as the primary method for managing dust.[11] Fans can, however, be useful as a supplement to other control methods. Use fans in enclosed areas, such as bathrooms, where dust would build up due to poor air circulation.

For the best effect, set an exhaust fan (the bigger, the better) in an open window or external doorway. Position the saw nearby, so that the fan captures dust and blows it outside. Avoid positioning employees between the saw and the fan. Also, avoid positioning employees near the exhausted air. An exhaust fan works best if a second window or door across the room is open to allow fresh air to enter.

Considerations

While dust control using vacuum dust collection may be an attractive option in some circumstances, it is not as effective as wet cutting for controlling respirable dust. Respiratory protection may still be needed to reduce employee exposures to levels of 0.1 mg/m³ or less when using vacuum dust collection.

Provide employees with respiratory protection until air sampling indicates that their exposure is adequately controlled.

Compressed Air
The use of compressed air to clean surfaces or clothing is strongly discouraged. Using compressed air to clean work surfaces or clothing can significantly increase employee exposure, especially in enclosed and semi-enclosed spaces. Cleaning should be performed with a HEPA-filtered vacuum or by wet methods.

Respiratory Protection and Engineering Control Evaluation

Using a stationary saw without engineering controls can cause exposure to respirable silica to reach 2.0 mg/m3 or higher. Therefore, it is important to utilize effective controls to reduce employee exposures. Wet methods present the best choice for suppressing dust while cutting with stationary saws. Studies indicate that effective wet methods can reduce exposures below 0.05 mg/m^3, as an 8-hour TWA. Stationary saws can be purchased with water-fed equipment, or existing saws can be retrofitted with water-fed attachments. Respiratory protection should not be necessary when using effective wet methods.

In situations where wet methods may not be appropriate or feasible, vacuum dust collection may be an alternative control option. However, data indicate that vacuum dust collection alone can only reduce exposures to 0.4 mg/m^3. Therefore, to supplement this control option, employees need to wear a properly fitted, NIOSH-approved half-facepiece or disposable respirator equipped with an N-, R-, or P-95 filter. A half-facepiece or disposable respirator can be used for exposures up to 1.0 mg/m^3.

In any workplace where respirators are necessary to protect the health of the employee, or whenever respirators are required by the employer, the employer must establish and implement a written respiratory protection program with worksite-specific procedures and elements, including the selection of respirators, medical evaluations of employees, fit testing, proper usage, maintenance and care, cleaning and disinfecting, proper air quality/quantity and training (see 29 CFR 1926.103).

Other employees in close proximity to the work operations where silica dust is generated may also need respiratory protection if effective controls are not implemented. The level of respiratory protection is dependent on the employee's silica exposure, which varies depending on factors in the work environment (such as enclosed, semi-enclosed, or open spaces and/or multiple operations generating silica dust), environmental conditions (such as wind direction and speed), and the percentage of silica found in the material.

Construction sites often involve many operations occurring simultaneously that can generate respirable silica dust. Therefore, it is important and necessary to utilize effective controls (such as wet methods and/or vacuum dust collection) in order to minimize total exposures to silica-exposed tool operators or potential exposures to other employees.

Employers should conduct exposure monitoring periodically while controls are being used to ensure that the controls are working properly and that the appropriate level of respiratory protection is being used.

For more information on how to determine proper respiratory protection, visit OSHA's Web site at www.osha.gov. NIOSH's Web site also provides information on respirators at www.cdc.gov/niosh.

References

ACGIH. 2007. Industrial Ventilation, A Manual of Recommended Practice, 26th Edition. American Conference of Governmental Industrial Hygienists, Cincinnati, OH.

ACGIH. 2008. Threshold limit values for chemical substances and physical agents and biological exposure indices. American Conference of Governmental Industrial Hygienists, Cincinnati, OH.

Croteau, G.A. 2000. The effect of local exhaust ventilation controls on dust exposures during masonry activities. MS Thesis. University of Washington. June, 2000.

Croteau, G.A. Guffey, S.E., Flanagan, M.E. and Seixas NS. 2002. The effect of local exhaust ventilation controls on dust exposures during concrete cutting and grinding activities. Am Ind Hygiene Assn J. 63:458-467. July/August.

ERG. 2000. Site visit report - Masonry Training Facility A. Eastern Research Group, Inc., Arlington, VA. September, 2000.

Heitbrink, W.A. and Watkins, D.S. 2001. The effect of exhaust flow rate upon the respirable dust emissions for tuckpointing operations. In: In-Depth Study Report: Control Technology for Crystalline Silica Exposures in Construction. U.S. Department of Health and Human Services, Centers for Disease Control and Prevention, National Institute for Occupational Safety and Health. ECTB No. 247-18.

Heitbrink, W. and Collingwood, S. 2005. Protecting Tuckpointing Workers from Silica Dust: Draft Recommendations for Ventilated Grinder. The Center to Protect Workers' Rights (CPWR). www.cpwr.com

Lofgren, D.J. 1993. Silica exposure for concrete workers and masons. Appl Occup Environ Hygiene 8(10):832-836. October, 1993.

NIOSH. 1996. Preventing Silicosis and Deaths in Construction Workers. Publication No. 96-112. National Institute for Occupational Safety and Health.

NIOSH. 1999a. Control technology and exposure assessment for occupational exposure to crystalline silica: Case 16 - Wet Cutting of Concrete Masonry Units, File No. ECTB 233-116c. National Institute for Occupational Safety and Health, Cincinnati, OH. October, 1999.

NIOSH. 1999b. Control technology and exposure assessment for occupational exposure to crystalline silica: Case 18 - Cutting Brick and Concrete Masonry Units. ECTB 233-118c. National Institute for Occupational Safety and Health, Cincinnati, OH. November, 1999.

NIOSH. 2002. Pocket guide to chemical hazards. Pub. No. 2002-140. National Institute for Occupational Safety and Health, Cincinnati, OH. June, 2002.

OSHA. 1996. Ground-fault protection on construction sites. Occupational Safety and Health Administration, Office of Training and Education. May, 1996.

OSHA Case Files (Special Emphasis Program Inspection Reports from 1996-1998).

Shields, C. 2000. Database: Silica dust exposures associated with construction activities (version date: September 14, 2000). Occupational Safety and Health Administration, North Aurora Office, IL.

Technical Notes

[1] Laboratories have not used particle counting for crystalline silica analysis for many years. Exposure data is now reported gravimetrically. However, OSHA's construction PEL for crystalline silica, established in 1971, is still listed as a particle-count value. (See Appendix E to OSHA's National Emphasis Program for Crystalline Silica, CPL 03-00-007, for a detailed discussion of the conversion factor used to transform gravimetric measurements to particle-count values). In this guidance, OSHA is using the general industry PEL (0.1 mg/m^3 of respirable quartz as an 8-hour time-weighted average) as a benchmark to describe the effectiveness of control measures. The benchmark is approximately equivalent to the general industry silica PEL. Other organizations suggest more stringent levels. For example, the National Institute for Occupational Safety and Health (NIOSH) recommends that respirable crystalline silica exposures be limited to 0.05 mg/m^3 as a 10-hour time-weighted average (NIOSH, 2002). The American Conference of Governmental Industrial Hygienists (ACGIH) recommends that respirable crystalline silica exposures be limited to 0.025 mg/m^3 as an 8-hour time-weighted average (ACGIH, 2008).

[2] Some employers use a hose connected to an external water source to provide a continuous flow of fresh water in place of recirculated water. This eliminates the need for pumps and filters, but requires substantially more water and produces more runoff.

[3] Nine results contained in NIOSH, 1999a and 1999b; Shields, 2000; ERG, 2000; and OSHA Case Files. The one exception was a result of 0.1 mg/m3.

[4] The respirable silica concentration in the employee's breathing zone during the period monitored was 2.8 mg/m^3.

[5] Two results associated with exceptionally short sampling periods (a 56-minute result of 7.5 mg/m^3 and a 2-minute result of 3.1 mg/m^3) were excluded from this average, but included in the subsequent text on periods of intensive cutting.

[6] Some saws come set up for both water-feed and vacuum dust collection for better employee protection in all situations.

[7] For the system tested by Croteau et al. (2002), an airflow of 70 cubic feet per minute (CFM) through the vacuum controlled respirable dust better than 30 CFM. ACGIH (2007) recommends a still higher airflow of 25 CFM per inch of blade diameter (equivalent to 236 CFM for the saw tested). Low airflow can cause ducts to clog. For abrasive wheel saws with vacuum dust collection, ACGIH recommends a minimum airflow velocity of 4,000 feet per minute (FPM) through ducts to prevent dust from settling. For a typical 2-inch diameter vacuum hose, 75 to 90 CFM will achieve that duct velocity. Larger hoses are acceptable for larger vacuums that draw more CFM of air. For example, 350 CFM of airflow would create the recommended air velocity in a 4-inch duct.

[8] With careful experimentation, it is possible to construct a booth that controls exposures to levels below OSHA's limits. First, make adjustments to control visible dust escaping from the front of the booth. Then, conduct air sampling (preferably under a variety of cutting conditions) to confirm that the booth will also protect the operator from respirable sized particles.

[9] Booth dimensions were approximately 6 feet by 6.5 feet by 3.5 feet, with a 36-inch fan. Air moved through the open face of the booth at an average velocity of 250 feet per minute (FPM), consistent with ACGIH's recommendation for abrasive cut-off saw booths.

[10] Sampling periods at this site were of 318 to 462 minutes duration.

Handheld Masonry Saws

This section covers gas-, air-, electric- and hydraulic-powered handheld masonry saws. The term "silica" used in this document refers to respirable crystalline silica.

Employee operating a handheld masonry saw without the use of appropriate dust controls. (Photo courtesy of OSHA.)

Introduction

Exposure to fine particles of silica has been shown to cause silicosis, a serious and sometimes fatal lung disease. Construction employees who inhale fine particles of silica may be at risk of developing this disease. Employees produce dusts containing silica when they cut, grind, crush, or drill construction materials such as concrete, masonry, tile and rock. The small particles easily become suspended in the air and, when inhaled, penetrate deep into employees' lungs.

Studies show that using a handheld masonry saw to cut bricks, concrete blocks and similar materials can result in hazardous levels of airborne silica if measures are not taken to reduce dust emissions. Operating a handheld masonry saw outdoors without dust controls can produce silica exposures as high as 14 times the Occupational Safety and Health Administration's (OSHA) benchmark of 0.1 mg/m³ (milligrams per cubic meter of air) as an 8-hour time-weighted average (TWA), an exposure approximately equivalent to OSHA's general industry permissible exposure limit (PEL) for construction (OSHA Case Files).[1] Short-term exposures or exposures from operating saws indoors can be significantly higher (up to 10 mg/m³).

Visible and Respirable Dust

Visible dust contains large particles that are easy to see. The tiny, respirable-sized particles (those that can get into the deep lung) containing silica pose the greatest hazard and are not visible. Most dust-generating construction activities produce a mixture of visible and respirable particles.

Do use visible dust as a general guide for improving dust suppression efforts. If you see visible dust being generated, emissions of respirable silica are probably too high. Measures that control tool-generated dust at the source usually reduce *all* types of particle emissions, including respirable particles.

Do not rely *only* on visible dust to assess the extent of the silica hazard. There may be airborne respirable dust present that is not visible to the naked eye.

This section describes methods available to reduce employees' exposures to silica when using handheld masonry saws. Walk-behind saws are addressed in a separate section for walk-behind surface preparation tools. OSHA encourages you to use this information to evaluate or improve system performance to reduce dust emissions. Technical notes are found at the end of this section and are referenced throughout the text.

Two main methods exist to control silica dust while operating a handheld masonry saw: (1) wet cutting and (2) vacuum dust collection.

Wet cutting, when used properly, is an effective way to reduce employee exposures to silica dust and in most cases maintains exposures below the allowable limit. ***Vacuum dust collection*** can significantly reduce silica levels, but may not reliably keep them below 0.1 mg/m³ as an 8-hour TWA.

When applying water to the blade, exposures of handheld saw operators to silica are considerably reduced. (Photo courtesy of OSHA.)

Silica Dust Control Measures

Wet Cutting

Water-fed handheld saws that are gasoline-powered, air-powered, electric-powered and hydraulic-powered are commercially available (Stihl, 2001; Diamond Products, 2001; Partner Industrial Products, 2001). Water can be supplied to the saws either with a pressurized portable water supply or with a constant water source, for example, a hose connected to a municipal water supply.

Wet cutting is the most effective method for controlling silica dust generated during sawing because it controls the exposure at its source. Dust that is wet is less able to become or remain airborne. The effectiveness of both a pressurized portable water supply and a constant water supply was evaluated by Thorpe et al. (1999). They found that respirable dust levels were reduced by up to 94 percent for pressurized portable water supply systems and up to 96 percent for a constant supplying water source. NIOSH reported that an employee dry cutting on concrete outdoors was exposed to 1.5 mg/m^3 of silica as an 8-hour TWA (NIOSH, 1999c). A reduction of 96 percent in respirable dust for this employee would have resulted in exposure around 0.06 mg/m^3 if the employee switched to a wet method.

Maintaining a Water-Feed System

- Check to ensure that hoses are securely connected and not cracked or broken.
- Adjust nozzles to ensure that water is directed so that the maximum amount reaches the cutting area while still cooling the blade.
- Dispose of water containing silica in a way that prevents the silica from becoming resuspended in the air. If the silica is allowed to become airborne, it can contribute to employee exposures.
- Consult the manufacturer for equipment operating specifications and recommendations that apply to the specific saw model including electrical fault protection, such as a ground-fault circuit interrupter (GFCI).

Maintenance. To minimize dust emissions from saws equipped for wet cutting, keep hoses and nozzles in excellent operating condition. Regular saw maintenance reduces silica exposures and ensures optimal operation of the equipment. Saws and dust control devices should be on a routine maintenance schedule.

Freezing Temperatures. Freezing temperatures complicate the use of water.[2] Consider heating the local work area, if practical, to prevent ice from forming in the water-feed system. Large portable

heating units are commonly used to heat commercial and sometimes road and highway projects. Drain the system when not in use. If water freezes on the ground, chip away the ice or use deicing compounds or sand to control the slipping hazard.

Electrical Safety. Use ground-fault circuit interrupters (GFCIs) and watertight, sealable electrical connectors for electric tools and equipment on construction sites (OSHA, 1996). These features are particularly important to employee safety in wet or damp areas, such as where water is used to control dust. Although an assured equipment grounding conductor program is an acceptable alternative to GFCIs, OSHA recommends that employers use GFCIs where possible because they provide better protection for employees. (See 29 CFR 1926.404(b)(1) for OSHA's ground-fault protection requirements.)

Vacuum Dust Collection Systems

Handheld saws can also be equipped with vacuum dust collection (VDC) systems. Saws equipped with VDC systems can be effective in controlling respirable silica exposure. One study by Thorpe et al. (1999) found that a VDC system on the handheld saw reduced mean respirable concrete dust concentrations from 8 mg/m^3 to 0.7 mg/m^3. This represents an 88 percent reduction in respirable concrete dust. However, this study used a dust collection device (exterior hood) that may not be commercially available.

Other studies have shown that handheld VDC-equipped saws do not offer a reliable reduction in exposure to dust. Two studies, Croteau (2000) and Croteau et al. (2002), tested a handheld saw equipped with a VDC system exhausting at 70 cubic feet per minute (CFM). Unfortunately, this system did not reduce respirable silica exposure. The studies concluded that the shape of the opening on the dust collection device was not effective in capturing the dust being emitted from the rotating blade. In some cases, handheld saw and VDC system combinations might require the rotation of the blade to be reversed to optimize dust collection (USF Surface Preparation Group, 2002). However, such modifications generally must be performed by the manufacturer.

NIOSH obtained 8-hour TWA respirable silica results between 0.117 and 0.388 mg/m^3 for six employees at two separate construction sites (NIOSH, 1999a; NIOSH, 1999b). The employees used no dust controls on this worksite. However, they worked outdoors and used the handheld saw intermittently. The rest of the time on the worksite was spent on activities that did not generate respirable crystalline silica. If the handheld saw that was used intermittently had been equipped with a VDC system, dust levels could have been reduced 75 percent, resulting in exposures between 0.03 mg/m³ and 0.01 mg/m³.

Although data on VDC-equipped handheld saws used indoors were not available, one measurement obtained from an employee cutting indoors without a VDC system yielded a silica exposure of 10.3 mg/m³. The employee was a plumber cutting concrete floors around drains in a 16-story building. Even if the employee achieved an 88 percent reduction in dust exposure using the VDC system described by Thorpe et al. (1999), exposure still would have exceeded 1.0 mg/m³.

Compressed Air

The use of compressed air to clean surfaces or clothing is strongly discouraged. Using compressed air to clean work surfaces or clothing can significantly increase employee exposure, especially in enclosed and semi-enclosed spaces. Cleaning should be performed with a HEPA-filtered vacuum or by wet methods.

Recommendations for Vacuum Dust Collection Systems. The American Conference of Governmental Industrial Hygienists (ACGIH) recommends airflow of 25 CFM per inch of blade diameter. If airflow is too low, the hose may clog with particulate matter. A study by Croteau et al. (2002), which tested an abrasive wheel saw, found a 2-inch diameter vacuum hose and a flow rate of 75 to 90 CFM achieved an air velocity of 4,000 feet per minute (FPM). Achieving this air velocity prevented particulate matter from settling in the hose. If the VDC provides a higher flow rate, then it is acceptable to use a larger hose.

VDC systems can be purchased as a kit. These kits should include a dust collector (exterior hood), vacuum, vacuum hose and filter(s). The components of a VDC system are discussed below.

- *Dust collector (exterior hood)*: In most cases, this is a retrofit on the saw; therefore, be sure to follow the manufacturer's instructions when installing the device.

- *Vacuum*: Choose a vacuum with the appropriate power and capacity for your job.

- *Vacuum hose*: A flow rate of 80 CFM is best maintained with a 1½- to 2-inch diameter hose. If the diameter is larger, the airflow velocity of the vacuum will be reduced. If the diameter is smaller, airflow resistance will be higher. Airflow

resistance also increases with hose length; excessively long hoses should be avoided. Many HEPA-filtered vacuum system kits include a variety of hose sizes for different tool applications.

- *Filters*: Double filtration is important. The use of a high-efficiency particulate air (HEPA) filter is critical to prevent the escape of respirable silica dust from the vacuum exhaust. HEPA filters are at least 99.97 percent efficient in removing fine dust particles from the air. A prefilter or cyclonic separator in addition to a HEPA filter will improve vacuum efficiency and extend the service life of the more costly HEPA filter. A cyclonic separator removes large particles that are capable of overloading or clogging the filter. (Heitbrink and Collingwood, 2005).[3]

- *Systematic cleaning*: Choose a vacuum equipped with a back-pulse filter cleaning cycle. Such auto-cleaning mechanisms will reduce the time required for vacuum maintenance and improve the overall efficiency of the dust collection system. If the vacuum does not have an auto-cleaning mechanism, the employee can periodically turn the vacuum cleaner on and off. This allows the bag to collapse and causes the prefilter cake to dislodge from the filter.

- *Monitoring VDC efficiency*: Purchasing a dust collection system equipped with a static pressure gauge allows the employee to monitor the system's efficiency. Systems lacking a static pressure gauge can be monitored visually. If a dust plume increases and becomes more visible where the dust collector (exterior hood) meets the working surface, the system is not working efficiently. When relying on this technique to monitor the efficiency of the dust collection system, try to locate the vacuum as far away from adjacent employees as possible to help limit their exposure to silica (Heitbrink and Collingwood, 2005).

Work Practice Controls to Enhance Vacuum Effectiveness. Studies have shown that the effectiveness of vacuum dust collection systems is enhanced by the use of proper work practices (NIOSH, 1999a; NIOSH, 1999b; NIOSH 1999c; Croteau et al., 2002). However, use of these work techniques without a dust collection system will not substantially reduce dust exposures.

With any type of vacuum system, employee protection from respirable dust is only as good as the filter in the vacuum. The less efficient the filter, the more respirable dust will pass through with the vacuum exhaust air. Locating the vacuum as far from employees as possible is one way to help limit exposure.

For optimal dust collection, the following measures are recommended:

- Keep the vacuum hose clear and free of debris, kinks and tight bends. Maintain the vacuum at peak performance to ensure adequate airflow through the dust collector (exterior hood) and vacuum hoses.

- On vacuums with back-pulse filter cleaning systems, activate the system frequently (several times per day). Empty collection bags and vacuums as frequently as necessary. Dispose of collected dust in a way that prevents it from becoming resuspended in the air.

- For best results, set up a regular schedule for filter cleaning and maintenance. For example, institute a rule to clean the filter or change the bag at each break. This will prevent pressure loss and ensure that exhaust airflow stays constant on the VDC system.

- Remember, the absence of visible dust does not necessarily mean that employees are adequately protected from silica exposure.

Fans

Fans are not effective dust control devices when used as the sole control method and should not be used as the primary method for managing dust. Fans can, however, be useful as a supplement to other control methods. Use fans in enclosed areas, such as bathrooms, where dust may build up due to poor air circulation.

For the best effect, set an exhaust fan (the bigger, the better) in an open window or external doorway. Position the saw nearby, so that the fan captures dust and blows it outside. Avoid positioning employees between the saw and the fan. Also, avoid positioning employees near the exhausted air. An exhaust fan works best if a second window or door across the room is opened to allow fresh air to enter.

Considerations

While dust control using VDC may be an attractive option in some circumstances, it is not as effective as wet cutting for controlling respirable dust. Respiratory protection may still be needed to reduce employee exposures below 0.1 mg/m³ as an 8-hour TWA when using VDC.

Provide employees with respiratory protection until air sampling demonstrates that their exposure is adequately controlled.

Respiratory Protection and Engineering Control Evaluation

Using a handheld saw without engineering controls can cause exposures to respirable crystalline silica to reach 1.5 mg/m³ during outdoor operations, with indoor exposures being significantly higher (up to 10 mg/m³). Therefore, effective controls are needed to reduce employee exposures below 0.1 mg/m³ as an 8-hour TWA.

Effective wet methods provide the most reliable control for silica dust and are invaluable in keeping silica levels below 0.1 mg/m3 as an 8-hour TWA. Most handheld saws are manufactured with water-fed equipment. Employees who use saws that do not include water-fed equipment should apply water directly to the cutting point. Water should be applied at a minimum rate of *0.13 gallons per minute* to ensure adequate dust suppression outdoors. When effective wet methods are used outdoors, it is unlikely that supplemental respiratory protection will be needed (Thorpe et al., 1999).

The use of wet methods during indoor operations can reduce silica exposures, but may not reduce exposures below 0.1 mg/m³. However, when wet methods are used, exposures will not likely exceed 1.0 mg/m³. When wet methods cannot reduce exposures below 0.1 mg/m³, employees should supplement them with a NIOSH-approved half-facepiece or disposable respirator equipped with an N-, R-, or P-95 filter.

In situations where wet methods may not be appropriate or feasible, VDC systems may be an alternative control option. Current data suggest that the reduction in silica offered by VDC systems is variable. For outdoor operations, using effective VDC may reduce exposures below 1.0 mg/m³, but not necessarily below 0.1 mg/m³. Therefore, employees may need to wear a properly fitted, NIOSH-approved half-facepiece or a disposable respirator equipped with an N-, R- or P-95 filter (see 29 CFR 1926.103).

In any workplace where respirators are necessary to protect the health of the employee, or whenever respirators are required by the employer, the employer must establish and implement a written respiratory protection program with work-site-specific procedures and elements. These should include the selection of respirators, medical evaluations of employees, fit testing, proper usage, maintenance and care, cleaning and disinfecting, proper air quality/quantity and training (see 29 CFR 1926.103).

Exposure control data are limited regarding the use of a VDC system during indoor sawing operations. A handheld saw equipped with a VDC system cannot be relied upon solely to reduce exposures below 0.1 mg/m^3; therefore, employees may need to wear a full-facepiece respirator equipped with an N-, R-, or P-95 filter (see 29 CFR 1926.103).

Other employees in close proximity to the work operations where silica dust is generated may also need respiratory protection if effective controls are not implemented. The level of respiratory protection is dependent on the employee's silica exposure, which varies depending on factors in the work environment (such as enclosed, semi-enclosed, or open spaces and/or multiple operations generating silica dust), environmental conditions (such as wind direction and speed) and the percentage of silica found in the material.

Construction sites often involve many operations occurring simultaneously that can generate respirable silica dust. Therefore, it is important and necessary to utilize effective controls (such as wet-methods and/or vacuum dust collection) in order to minimize total exposures to silica-exposed tool operators or potential exposures to other employees.

Employers should conduct exposure monitoring periodically while controls are being used to ensure that the controls are working properly and that the appropriate level of respiratory protection is being used.

For more information on how to determine proper respiratory protection, visit OSHA's Web site at www.osha.gov. NIOSH's Web site also provides information on respirators at www.cdc.gov/niosh.

References

ACGIH. 2001. Industrial Ventilation, A Manual of Recommended Practice, 24th Edition. American Conference of Governmental Industrial Hygienists, Cincinnati, OH.

ACGIH. 2008. Threshold limit values for chemical substances and physical agents and biological exposure indices. American Conference of Governmental Industrial Hygienists, Cincinnati, OH.

Croteau, G.A. 2000. The effect of local exhaust ventilation controls on dust exposures during masonry activities. MS Thesis. University of Washington. June, 2000.

Croteau, G.A., Guffey, S.E., Flanagan, M.E. and Seixas, N.S. 2002. The effect of local exhaust ventilation controls on dust exposures during concrete cutting and grinding activities. Am Ind Hygiene Assn J 63:458-467. July/August, 2002.

Diamond Products. 2001. SpeediCut cut-off saws. http://diamondproducts.com. Accessed September 8, 2008.

Heitbrink, W.A. and Watkins, D.S. 2001. The effect of exhaust flow rate upon the respirable dust emissions for tuckpointing operations. In: In-Depth Study Report: Control Technology for Crystalline Silica Exposures in Construction. U.S. Department of Health and Human Services, Centers for Disease Control and Prevention, National Institute for Occupational Safety and Health. ECTB No. 247-18.

Heitbrink, W. and Collingwood, S. 2005. Protecting Tuckpointing Workers from Silica Dust: Draft Recommendations for Ventilated Grinder. The Center to Protect Workers' Rights (CPWR). www.cpwr.com

NIOSH. 1995. Environmental surveillance report: Concrete Coring, Inc., Enon, OH. U.S. Department of Health and Human Services, Public Health Service, Centers for Disease Control and Prevention, National Institute for Occupational Safety and Health, Division of Respiratory Disease Studies, Morgantown, WV.

NIOSH. 1996. Alert: request for assistance in preventing silicosis and deaths in construction workers. DHHS (NIOSH) Publication No. 96-112. U.S. Department of Health and Human Services, Public Health Service, Centers for Disease Control and Prevention, National Institute for Occupational Safety and Health, Division of Physical Sciences and Engineering, Cincinnati, OH.

NIOSH. 1999a. Control technology and exposure assessment for occupational exposure to crystalline silica: Case 17 - dry cutting of concrete masonry units. U.S. Department of Health and Human Services, Public Health Service, Centers for Disease Control and Prevention, National Institute for Occupational Safety and Health, Division of Physical Sciences and Engineering, Cincinnati, OH. ECTB 233-117c.

NIOSH. 1999b. Control technology and exposure assessment for occupational exposure to crystalline silica: Case 18 - cutting brick and concrete masonry units. U.S. Department of Health and Human Services, Public Health Service, Centers for Disease Control and Prevention, National Institute for Occupational Safety and Health, Division of Physical Sciences and Engineering, Cincinnati, OH. ECTB 233-118c.

NIOSH. 1999c. Control technology and exposure assessment for occupational exposure to crystalline silica: Case 21 - non-residential construction. U.S. Department of Health and Human Services, Public Health Service, Centers for Disease Control and Prevention, National Institute for Occupational Safety and Health, Division of Physical Sciences and Engineering, Cincinnati, OH. ECTB 233-121c.

NIOSH. 2002. Pocket guide to chemical hazards. Pub. No. 2002-140. National Institute for Occupational Safety and Health, Cincinnati, OH. June, 2002.

OSHA. 1996. Ground-fault protection on construction sites. Occupational Safety and Health Administration, Office of Training and Education. May, 1996.

OSHA Case Files (Special Emphasis Program Inspection Reports from 1996-1998).

Partner Industrial Products. 2001. The Partner wet cutting system. http://www.partnerusa.com. Accessed September 8, 2008.

Shields, C. 2000. Database: Silica dust exposures associated with construction activities (version date: September 14, 2000). Occupational Safety and Health Administration, North Aurora Office, IL.

Stihl. 2001. Cutquick® cut-off machine accessories. http://www.stihlusa.com. Accessed September 8, 2008.

Thorpe, A., Ritchie, A.S., Gibson, M.J. and Brown, R.C. 1999. Measurements of the effectiveness of dust control on cut-off saws used in the construction industry. Annals of Occup Hygiene 43 (7) 1443-1456. July, 1999.

Trakumas, S., Willeke, K., Reponen, T., Grinshpun, S.A. and Freidman, W. 2001. Comparison of filter bag, cyclonic, and wet dust collection methods in vacuum cleaners. Am Ind Hygiene Assn J 62:573-583.

USF Surface Preparation Group. 2000b. Sawtec JS-90. www.surfacepreparation.com Accessed September 8, 2008.

USF Surface Preparation Group. 2002. Personal communication between USF and Laura Lewis of ERG, Inc. January 28, 2002.

Zalk, D. 2000. Exposure assessment strategy for the reduction of airborne silica during jackhammering activities. Presentation. American Industrial Hygiene Conference and Exposition, Orlando, FL. May 20-25, 2000.

Technical Notes

[1] Laboratories have not used particle counting for crystalline silica analysis for many years. Exposure data is now reported gravimetrically. However, OSHA's construction PEL for crystalline silica, established in 1971, is still listed as a particle-count value. (See Appendix E to OSHA's National Emphasis Program for Crystalline Silica, CPL 03-00-007, for a detailed discussion of the conversion factor used to transform gravimetric measurements to particle-count values). In this guidance, OSHA is using 0.1 mg/m^3 of respirable quartz as an 8-hour time-weighted average as a benchmark to describe the effectiveness of control measures. The benchmark is approximately equivalent to the general industry silica PEL. Other organizations suggest lower levels. For example, the National Institute for Occupational Safety and Health (NIOSH) recommends that respirable crystalline silica exposures be limited to 0.05 mg/m^3 as a 10-hour time-weighted average (NIOSH, 2002). The American Conference of Governmental Industrial Hygienists (ACGIH) recommends that respirable crystalline silica exposures be limited to 0.025 mg/m^3 as an 8-hour time-weighted average (ACGIH, 2008).

[2] Some saws come set up for both water-feed and vacuum dust collection for better employee protection in all situations.

[3] For the system tested by Croteau et al. (2002), an airflow of 90 cubic feet per minute (CFM) through the vacuum controlled respirable dust better than 70 CFM. ACGIH (2001) recommends a still higher airflow of 25 CFM per inch of blade diameter (equivalent to 236 CFM for the saw tested). Low airflow can cause ducts to clog. For abrasive wheel saws with vacuum dust collection, ACGIH recommends a minimum airflow velocity of 4,000 feet per minute (FPM) through ducts to prevent dust from settling. For a typical 2-inch diameter vacuum hose, 75 to 90 CFM will achieve that duct velocity. Larger hoses are acceptable for larger vacuums that draw more CFM of air. For example, 350 CFM of airflow would create the recommended air velocity in a 4-inch duct.

Hand-Operated Grinders

This section covers electric- and pneumatic-hand-operated grinders used for surface finishing and cutting slots. Angle grinders used for tuckpointing are addressed in a separate section. The term "silica" used in this document refers to respirable crystalline silica.

Introduction

Employees produce dusts containing silica when they grind on concrete and similar materials. The grinders' abrasive action generates fine particles that easily become suspended in the air and, when inhaled, penetrate deep into employees' lungs. Exposure to fine particles of silica has been shown to cause silicosis, a serious and sometimes fatal lung disease. Construction employees who inhale fine particles of silica may be at risk of developing this disease This section discusses the methods available to reduce employee exposures to silica during grinding activities.

Data compiled by the Occupational Safety and Health Administration (OSHA) indicate that, among employees who grind concrete, most are exposed to silica at levels that exceed OSHA's benchmark of 0.1 mg/m³ (milligrams of silica per cubic meter of air) as an 8-hour time-weighted average (TWA), an exposure approximately equivalent to OSHA's general industry permissible exposure limit (PEL).[1] In fact, on average, grinder operators' silica exposures (along with those of tuckpointers) are among the highest in the construction industry.[2] More than half of all grinder operators experience silica exposures above 0.2 mg/m³ (milligrams per cubic meter of air).[3] During periods of intensive grinding, concrete finishers' exposures can exceed 1.2 mg/m³ outdoors and 4.5 mg/m³ indoors (Lofgren, 1993; OSHA Case Files).[4]

Vacuum dust collection systems are used to reduce silica dust during concrete grinding operations. Vacuum methods can significantly reduce dust emissions, but thus far have not been shown to reliably keep silica levels below 0.1 mg/m³ as an 8-hour time-weighted average (TWA).

Wet grinding is highly effective in reducing silica exposures. Handheld water-fed grinding equipment is commercially available for concrete applications, granite grinding, and polishing operations. Conventional grinding equipment can be retrofitted to add a water-feed capability.[5]

Using a grinder in poorly controlled conditions. (Photo courtesy of OSHA Directorate of Construction.)

Adjustments in work methods and equipment, when possible, can lower exposure levels. For example, the use of jigs to increase the distance between the employee and the point of work can reduce exposure levels. Modifications in construction work methods for pouring, casting, finishing and installing concrete can reduce the amount of grinding required, which, in turn, can lower exposures.

Visible and Respirable Dust

Visible dust contains large particles that are easy to see. The tiny, respirable-sized particles (those that can get into the deep lung) containing silica pose the greatest hazard and are not visible. Most dust-generating construction activities produce a mixture of visible and respirable particles.

Do use visible dust as a general guide for improving dust suppression efforts. If you see visible dust being generated, emissions of respirable silica are probably too high. Measures that control tool-generated dust at the source usually reduce *all* types of particle emissions, including respirable particles.

Do not rely *only* on visible dust to assess the extent of the silica hazard. There may be airborne respirable dust present that is not visible to the naked eye.

Silica Dust Control Measures

Vacuum Dust Collection Systems

Vacuum dust collection (VDC) systems for grinders include a shroud, which surrounds the grinding wheel, hose, filters and a vacuum to pull air through the shroud. Many manufacturers offer grinders with dust collection options. Employers may also purchase equipment to retrofit grinders for vacuum dust collection. The effectiveness of vacuum systems depends on several factors, including the user's technique, the surfaces being finished, and the efficiency of the dust collection system.

The addition of the shroud and vacuum hose may make it more difficult to work effectively while reaching overhead.

Recommendations for Vacuum Dust Collection Systems. The American Conference of Governmental Industrial Hygienists (ACGIH) recommends airflow of 25 cubic feet per minute (CFM) per inch of blade diameter (for example, a 4-inch grinder would need a vacuum with airflow of 100 CFM). If airflow is too low, the hose may clog with particulate matter. However, employers should be aware that rated airflows provided by manufacturers may be different from actual airflow once attached to the tool. A study by Croteau et al. (2002), which tested an abrasive wheel saw, found a 2-inch diameter vacuum hose and a flow rate of 75 CFM achieved an air velocity of 4,000 feet per minute (FPM). Achieving this air velocity prevented particulate matter from settling in the hose.

VDC systems can be purchased as a kit. These kits should include a grinder shroud (exterior hood), vacuum, vacuum hose, and filter(s). The components of a VDC system are discussed below.

- Grinder shroud (exterior hood): Employees should use a shroud appropriate for the grinder and wheel size.

- Vacuum: Choose a vacuum with the appropriate power and capacity for your job. Croteau et al. (2002) found a flow rate greater than 70 CFM to be effective.

- Vacuum hose: A 1½- to 2-inch diameter hose is usually best for smaller vacuums. If the diameter is larger, the airflow velocity of the vacuum will be reduced. If the diameter is smaller, airflow resistance will be higher. Airflow resistance also increases with hose length; excessively long hoses should be avoided.

- Filters: Double filtration is important. The use of a high-efficiency particulate air (HEPA) filter is critical to prevent the escape of respirable silica dust from the vacuum exhaust. HEPA filters are at least 99.97 percent efficient in removing fine dust particles from the air. A prefilter or cyclonic separator in addition to a HEPA filter will improve vacuum efficiency and extend the service life of the more costly HEPA filter. A cyclonic separator removes large particles that are capable of over-

loading or clogging the filter (Heitbrink and Collingwood, 2005).

- Systematic cleaning: Regular cleaning of the filter is critical to maintaining high airflow. Choose a vacuum equipped with a back-pulse filter cleaning cycle. Such auto-cleaning mechanisms will reduce the time required for vacuum maintenance and improve the overall efficiency of the dust collection system. If the vacuum does not have an auto-cleaning mechanism, the employee can periodically turn the vacuum cleaner on and off. This allows the bag to collapse and causes the prefilter cake to dislodge from the filter.

- Monitoring VDC efficiency: Purchasing a dust collection system equipped with a static pressure gauge allows the employee to monitor the system's efficiency. Systems lacking a static pressure gauge can be monitored visually. If a dust plume increases and becomes more visible where the shroud meets the working surface, the system is not working efficiently. When relying on this technique to monitor the efficiency of the dust collection system, try to locate the vacuum as far away from adjacent employees as possible to help limit their exposure to silica (Heitbrink and Collingwood, 2005).

System Maintenance. For optimal dust collection, the following measures are recommended:

- Keep the vacuum hose clear and free of debris, kinks and tight bends. Maintain the vacuum at peak performance to ensure adequate airflow through the shroud and ducts.

- On vacuums with back-pulse filter cleaning systems, activate the system frequently (several times per day). Empty collection bags and vacuums as frequently as necessary. Dispose of collected dust in a way that prevents it from becoming resuspended in the air.

- For best results, set up a regular schedule for filter cleaning and maintenance. For example, institute a rule to clean the filter or change the bag at each break. This will prevent pressure loss and ensure that exhaust airflow stays constant on the VDC system.

- Remember, the absence of visible dust does not necessarily mean that employees are adequately protected from silica exposure.

Grinder with attached VDC system. (Photo courtesy of OSHA Directorate of Construction.)

Fans

Fans are not effective dust control devices when used as the sole control method and should not be used as the primary method for managing dust. Fans can, however, be useful as a supplement to other control methods. Use fans in enclosed areas, such as bathrooms, where dust may build up due to poor air circulation.

For the best effect, set an exhaust fan (the bigger, the better) in an open window or external doorway. Position the grinder nearby, so the fan captures dust and blows it outside. Avoid positioning employees between the grinder and the fan. Also, avoid positioning employees near the exhausted air. An exhaust fan works best if a second window or door across the room is opened to allow fresh air to enter.

Example: A four-foot square fan is placed in a window exhausting to outside the building at maximum fan speed. The fan will have the strongest capture capability directly in front of the fan face, but this quickly drops off. At two feet away from the fan the capture capability is reduced to 50 percent and at four feet the capture capability is reduced to 7 percent of the capture capability at the fan face. If the distance between the grinding point and fan face is greater than the length of the fan side (4 feet), dust capture would probably not be effective (ACGIH, 2001).

Wet Grinding

Water provides excellent dust control during tasks involving abrasive action on concrete. When applied at the point where dust is generated, water wets the dust particles before they can become airborne.

Water-fed equipment is regularly used to control dust during granite and concrete grinding and pol-

ishing operations, as well as during concrete and masonry cutting with abrasive wheels. The wet methods consistently keep employee exposures below OSHA limits (Simcox et al., 1999; NIOSH, 1999). These tools include a nozzle or spout that provides a stream of water to the grinding wheel. For example, some equipment provides water through a hole in a hollow shaft or a nozzle at the edge of the wheel.

The National Institute for Occupational Safety and Health (NIOSH) reported that an employee reduced respirable dust levels by fitting an automatic water feed to a conventional handheld grinder and exhaust shroud system used for tuck-pointing (NIOSH, 2000a). Alternatively, a helper can apply water by hand using a spray nozzle (NIOSH, 1998). To be effective, the source must constantly supply water to the point of operation.

The use of water systems on similar tools used in the cut stone and stone products manufacturing industry has shown a reduction of exposures well below 0.1 mg/m^3 (NIOSH, 2000d and 2000e; and OSHA Case Files). It is reasonable to assume that such reductions can be achieved in the construction industry while using similar tools and control methods.

Wet methods have advantages, but require advance planning. The stone processing industry has shown that water-fed grinders function well to control dust even on uneven surfaces and near corners and edges (problem areas for vacuum dust collection equipment). Employees need training, however, to become comfortable working with water-fed grinders. A wet surface looks different from a dry one, and visibility during grinding may be obscured by water spray and slurry (OSHA Case Files). Slurry removal also requires an extra step in the cleaning process (for example, use of a wet-dry shop vacuum or rinsing the surface).[6] Nevertheless, wet methods offer reliable dust control during grinding.

Some surfaces might require extra cleaning (for example, with a pressure washer or hose and brush) after employees use wet methods. Avoid splashing concrete slurry on vehicles or other objects with specialty finishes.

Freezing Temperatures. Freezing temperatures complicate the use of water. Consider heating the local work area, if practical, to prevent ice from forming in the water-feed system. Large portable heating units are commonly used to heat commercial and sometimes road and highway projects. Drain the system when not in use. If water freezes on the ground, chip away the ice or use deicing compounds or sand to control the slipping hazard.

Electrical Safety. Use ground-fault circuit interrupters (GFCIs) and watertight, sealable electrical connectors for electric tools and equipment on construction sites (OSHA, 1996). These features are particularly important to employee safety in wet or damp areas, such as where water is used to control dust. Although an assured equipment grounding conductor program is an acceptable alternative to GFCIs, OSHA recommends that employers use GFCIs where possible because they afford better protection for employees. (See 29 CFR 1926.404(b)(1) for OSHA's ground-fault protection requirements.)

Adjustments in Work Methods

Employee Positioning

Where possible, exposures can be reduced if employees work at a greater distance from the grinding point. These reductions have been demonstrated for employees grinding on ceilings and for employees sanding drywall. Dust falls on employees who stand directly below the grinding point. If the grinder is attached to an adequately supported pole, the employee can manipulate the grinder at a distance from one side where the dust is less concentrated. While this method does not eliminate exposure, it can help reduce the amount of dust in the employee's breathing area (NIOSH, 1995; OSHA Case Files).

Grinding Wheel Size

A study comparing construction employees' respirable silica exposure at nine construction sites found that short-term exposure levels were about 30 percent higher for employees operating grinders with 7-inch wheels than for operators grinding with 4.5-inch wheels. Additionally, diamond wheels used for rougher, more aggressive grinding were associated with exposure levels approximately 60 percent higher than those associated with abrasive wheels used for fine finishing (Flanagan et al., 2003). Therefore, whenever possible, use a smaller rather than a larger wheel, and use the least aggressive tool that will do the job.

Construction Work Methods

Where practical, employers can reduce employees' silica exposures by utilizing construction methods and techniques that minimize the amount of grinding required. Examples include taking steps to minimize pouring/casting flaws and defects by ensuring tighter fitting forms, improved finishing, grinding

on pre-cast panels outdoors before installation inside, or using factory installed chase and grooves on pre-cast structural concrete (ERG, 2002; OSHA Case Files). Silica exposures may also be reduced if grinding is done while the concrete is still "green" (NIOSH, 2000b, NIOSH, 2000c). Additionally, for a given amount of material removed from a surface, less airborne dust will be generated if some of the material can be removed as larger chips instead of finely ground particles. An employee might use a hammer and chisel or power chipping equipment to remove most of the mass before using a grinder to smooth the surface.

Case Studies

The following case studies indicate silica exposure levels found under certain uncontrolled conditions, and show the effectiveness of controls in reducing silica exposures.

Case Studies - Silica Exposure Levels

Studies have shown that employees grinding concrete are exposed to potentially harmful levels of silica unless dust levels are controlled.

Indoors. *Case Study I:* Among data obtained by OSHA, grinder operators' silica exposures exceeded 1.0 mg/m³ during OSHA inspections reported for indoor construction sites. NIOSH reported an exposure level of 2.8 mg/m³ for a grinder operator finishing the walls, columns and floor inside an open-sided parking garage (NIOSH, 2001).

Some of the highest indoor results are associated with overhead work (grinding on ceilings). For example, OSHA reported exposures of 4.5, 4.5, 5.9, and 7.3 mg/m³ for four construction employees grinding slots and smoothing the ceiling of a mostly enclosed building (OSHA Case Files).

Outdoors. *Case Study II:* Exposures are somewhat lower outdoors, where dust can disperse more quickly, but results still indicate potentially harmful employee exposures. For example, data compiled by OSHA included results for three construction employees who primarily performed concrete grinding during the evaluation. The results indicate that the employees' silica exposures ranged from nearly 0.4 to 1.2 mg/m³ during the air sampling period. Even when results were averaged over their full shift, exposures were still 0.15 mg/m³ to 0.3 mg/m³ (Lofgren, 1993; OSHA Case Files).[7]

Other Employees in the Area. *Case Study III:* Silica dust released during uncontrolled grinding can affect other employees in the area. NIOSH collected area samples in the center of a room measuring 13 feet by 23 feet, while an employee used a grinder on the concrete walls. The area samples indicated that, over the course of a shift, a person (for example, an employee from another trade) could experience a silica exposure level of nearly 0.2 mg/m^3 by simply standing in the center of the room (NIOSH, 1998).[8]

Fortunately, bystander exposure can generally be reduced to levels well below OSHA limits by managing the dust. NIOSH found that when the grinder operator's exposure is reduced, bystander exposure drops as well. At the site mentioned above, the silica concentration in the middle of the room fell below the limit of detection when grinder operator exposures were reduced using either vacuum dust collection or wet-grinding methods (NIOSH, 1998).

Case Studies - Vacuum Dust Collection

Several case studies provide insights about employees' silica exposure when VDC systems are used to control dust emissions. These examples show that such systems significantly lower levels of airborne silica, but may not reliably reduce the grinder operator's exposures to levels below allowable limits.

Case Study IV: OSHA evaluated employees grinding on outdoor concrete pier structures for about 3 hours during bridge construction. Without controls, their daily average exposures to silica were 0.16 and 0.30 mg/m^3 as 8-hour TWAs.[9] OSHA then tested a shrouded grinder connected to a backpack vacuum with a HEPA filter. The silica exposure dropped to 0.02 mg/m^3 as an 8-hour TWA[10] (OSHA Case Files).

Case Study V: At another construction site, an employee operated a 7-inch grinder fitted with a dust collection shroud connected to a drum vacuum. Full-shift air samples collected on two days indicated a silica exposure level of 0.06 mg/m^3 on the first day and 0.11 mg/m^3 on the second day (OSHA Case Files). Exposure levels typically exceed these values when dust controls are not used.

Case Study VI: Researchers collected air samples for five days while one employee used various grinders fitted with a vacuum dust-collection shroud. The shroud was connected to a portable electric vacuum, which included a high-efficiency filter.[11] While the operator performed grinding on concrete walls inside a parking garage, breathing area exposure levels ranged from 0.06 to 0.2 mg/m^3 (Echt and Sieber, 2002; NIOSH, 2002b).

NIOSH (2001) obtained similar results from another employee testing various grinders, shrouds, and vacuums while smoothing concrete at a parking garage site. The three 6-hour samples collected on separate days indicated employee exposure levels of 0.17, 0.18, and 0.26 mg/m^3.[12]

The results reported in these case studies are notably lower than the exposure levels typically associated with uncontrolled concrete grinding. However, even when using a vacuum dust collection system, grinder operators' exposures often exceed 0.1 mg/m^3.

Case Studies - Fans

Case Study VII: A fan set up in the doorway of a small room was not adequate to remove the dust generated during grinding. No other methods were used to control dust. As a result, the grinder operator's exposure to silica was 1.4 mg/m^3 during a 2-hour period. In another indoor space where employees on a scaffold were grinding on a concrete wall, fans helped keep exposures at around 0.5 mg/m^3 for the periods evaluated (1.5 to 4 hours) (Lofgren, 1993).

Case Studies - Wet Methods

Case Study VIII: The results from two air samples for a grinder operator and helper showed that employees had low silica exposure when using water spray while smoothing concrete walls. The helper applied a spray of water from a hand-pump garden sprayer can filled with tap water. The investigators concluded that by constantly spraying the concrete just ahead of the grinder wheel, the employees reduced their exposure levels by 90 percent (NIOSH 1998).[13]

Case Studies - Employee Repositioning

Two studies suggest that employee positioning is an important determinant of silica exposure levels. The following examples show a tenfold difference in exposure recorded for employees using grinders attached to poles while grinding concrete ceilings at two (mostly enclosed) building sites. While employee position was a large factor, the type of work and the silica content of the concrete also accounted for some of the difference.

Case Study IX: At the first site, two grinder operators smoothed seams in a concrete ceiling using grinders on long extension jigs. The jigs were supported at an angle on rolling scaffolds. The operators manipulated the grinders from the bottom end of the jigs and were exposed to silica at levels of 0.184 and 0.415 mg/m³ (OSHA Case Files).[14]

Case Study X: Four operators at the second site ground utility slots and smoothed junctions in concrete ceilings, holding the grinders above their heads on short extensions fabricated from PVC pipe. The employees' exposure was exceptionally high, ranging from 4.5 to 7.2 mg/m³. In this case, the operators were removing more material (making more dust) and were positioned so that most of the dust fell directly onto them (OSHA Case Files).[15]

Compressed Air

The use of compressed air to clean surfaces or clothing is strongly discouraged. Using compressed air to clean work surfaces or clothing can significantly increase employee exposure, especially in enclosed and semi-enclosed spaces. Cleaning should be performed with a HEPA-filtered vacuum or by wet methods.

Respiratory Protection and Engineering Control Evaluation

Using a hand-operated grinder without engineering controls can cause exposures to respirable crystalline silica to reach 1.2 mg/m³ or higher while working outdoors and 4.5 mg/m³ or higher while working indoors. Effective wet methods are invaluable in keeping silica levels below 0.1 mg/m³ as an 8-hour TWA. When using effective wet methods, it is unlikely that respiratory protection will be needed.

In situations where wet methods may not be appropriate or feasible, VDC systems may be an alternative control option. Current data suggest that most grinding operations that utilize VDC systems usually exceed 0.1 mg/m³, but generally do not exceed 1.0 mg/m³. Therefore, to supplement the use of a VDC system, employees should wear a properly fitted, NIOSH-approved half-facepiece or disposable respirator equipped with an N-, R- or P-95 filter. A half-facepiece or disposable respirator can be used for protection at silica concentrations up to 1.0 mg/m³.

In any workplace where respirators are necessary to protect the health of the employee, or whenever respirators are required by the employer, the employer must establish and implement a written respiratory protection program with worksite-specific procedures and elements. These should include the selection of respirators, medical evaluations of employees, fit testing, proper usage, maintenance and care, cleaning and disinfecting, proper air quality/quantity and training (see 29 CFR 1926.103).

Where VDC systems and/or wet methods are not feasible, the employee may be subject to wearing a full-facepiece respirator equipped with an N-, R- or P-95 filter in conjunction with a respiratory protection program, which is also outlined in and must correspond with 29 CFR 1926.103. A full-facepiece respirator equipped with an N-, R- or P-95 is adequate for silica concentrations up to 5.0 mg/m³.

Other employees in close proximity to the work operations where silica dust is generated may also need respiratory protection if effective controls are not implemented. The level of respiratory protection is dependent on the employee's silica exposure, which varies depending on factors in the work environment (such as enclosed, semi-enclosed, or open spaces and/or multiple operations generating silica dust), environmental conditions (such as wind direction and speed), and the percentage of silica found in the material.

Construction sites often involve many operations occurring simultaneously that can generate respirable silica dust. Therefore, it is important and necessary to utilize effective controls (such as wet methods or VDC systems) in order to minimize total exposures to silica-exposed tool operators or potential exposures to other employees.

Employers should conduct exposure monitoring periodically while controls are being used to ensure that the controls are working properly and that the appropriate level of respiratory protection is being used.

For more information on how to determine proper respiratory protection, visit OSHA's Web site at www.osha.gov. NIOSH's Web site also provides information on respirators at www.cdc.gov/niosh.

References

ACGIH. 2001. Industrial Ventilation, A Manual of Recommended Practice, 24th Edition. American Conference of Governmental Industrial Hygienists, Cincinnati, OH.

ACGIH. 2008. Threshold limit values for chemical substances and physical agents and biological exposure indices. American Conference of Governmental Industrial Hygienists, Cincinnati, OH.

Akbar-Khanzadeh, F. and Brillhart, R.L. 2002. Respirable crystalline silica dust exposure during concrete finishing (grinding) using handheld grinders in the construction industry. Ann Occup Hygiene 46(3):341-346.

Croteau, G.A., Guffey, S.E., Flanagan, M.E. and Seixas, N.S. 2002. The effect of local exhaust ventilation controls on dust exposures during concrete cutting and grinding activities. Am Ind Hygiene Assn J. 63:458-467. July/August.

Echt, A. and Sieber, W.K. 2002. Control of silica exposure from hand tools in construction: Grinding concrete. Appl Occup Environ Hygiene 17(7):457-461. July, 2002.

ERG. 2002. Site visit report: Precast concrete product manufacturer facility B. Eastern Research Group, Inc. September 26, 2002.

Flanagan, M.E., Seixas, N., Majar, M., Camp, J. and Morgan, M. 2003. Silica dust exposures during selected construction activities. Am Ind Hygiene Assn J. 64(3):319-28. May-June, 2003.

Heitbrink, W.A. and Watkins, D.S. 2001. The effect of exhaust flow rate upon the respirable dust emissions for tuckpointing operations. In: In-Depth Study Report: Control Technology for Crystalline Silica Exposures in Construction. U.S. Department of Health and Human Services, Centers for Disease Control and Prevention, National Institute for Occupational Safety and Health. ECTB No. 247-18.

Heitbrink, W. and Collingwood, S. 2005. Protecting Tuckpointing Workers from Silica Dust: Draft Recommendations for Ventilated Grinder. The Center to Protect Workers' Rights (CPWR). www.cpwr.com

Lofgren, D.J. 1993. Silica exposure for concrete workers and masons. Appl. Occup. Environ. Hygiene 8(10):832-836. October, 1993.

NIOSH. 1995. In-depth survey report: A Laboratory Comparison of Conventional Drywall Sanding Techniques versus Commercially Available Control (ECTB 208-11a). National Institute for Occupational Safety and Health.

NIOSH. 1996. Preventing Silicosis and Deaths in Construction Workers. Dept. of Health and Human Services (National Institute for Occupational Safety and Health, Publication No. 96-112).

NIOSH. 1998. Environmental surveillance report: Construction site #16, Covington, KY. National Institute for Occupational Safety and Health, Morgantown, WV. June, 1998.

NIOSH. 1999. Control technology and exposure assessment for occupational exposure to crystalline silica: Case 16 - Wet Cutting of Concrete Masonry Units, File No. ECTB 233-116c. National Institute for Occupational Safety and Health, October, 1999.

NIOSH. 2000a. In-depth survey report: Control technology for crystalline silica exposures in construction: Exposures and preliminary control evaluation at various sites for Bricklayers Local #9, Pittsburgh, PA (ECTB 247-12). National Institute for Occupational Safety and Health, Cincinnati, OH. February, 2000.

NIOSH. 2000b. Control technology and exposure assessment for occupational exposure to crystalline silica: Case 25 – Concrete pipe manufacturing (ECTB 233-125c). National Institute for Occupational Safety and Health, Cincinnati, OH. March, 2000.

NIOSH. 2000c. Control technology and exposure assessment for occupational exposure to crystalline silica: Case 27 – Pre-cast concrete shape manufacturing (ECTB 233-127c). National Institute for Occupational Safety and Health, Cincinnati, OH. March, 2000.

NIOSH 2000d. Control technology and exposure assessment for occupational exposure to crystalline silica: Case - 31 – A granite shed. (ECTB 233-131c). National Institute for Occupational Safety and Health, Cincinnati, OH, August, 2000.

NIOSH 2000e. Control technology and exposure assessment for occupational exposure to crystalline silica: Case-32 – A granite shed. (ECTB 233-132c). National Institute for Occupational Safety and Health, Cincinnati OH. August, 2000.

NIOSH. 2001. In-depth survey report for four sites: Exposure to silica from hand tools in construction chipping, grinding and hand demolition at Frank Messer and Sons Construction Company, Lexington and Newport, KY, and Columbus and Springfield, OH (EPHB 247-15). National Institute for Occupational Safety and Health, Cincinnati, OH. April, 2001.

NIOSH. 2002a. In-depth survey report: Control of respirable dust and crystalline silica from grinding concrete at Frank Messer & Sons Construction, Newport, KY, and Baker Concrete Construction, Dayton, OH (EPHB 247-21). National Institute for Occupational Safety and Health, Cincinnati, OH. May, 2002.

NIOSH. 2002b. In-depth survey report: Control of silica exposure from hand tools in construction grinding concrete at Frank Messer and Sons Construction Company, Newport, KY (EPHB 247-15c). National Institute for Occupational Safety and Health, Cincinnati, OH. January, 2002.

NIOSH. 2002c. Pocket guide to chemical hazards. Pub. No. 2002-140. National Institute for Occupational Safety and Health, Cincinnati, OH.

OSHA. 1996. Ground-fault protection on construction sites. Occupational Safety and Health Administration, Office of Training and Education. May.

OSHA Case Files (Special Emphasis Program Inspection Reports from 1996-1998).

Simcox, N., Lofgren, D., Leons, J. and J. Camp. 1999. Case Studies: Silica Exposure During Granite Countertop Fabrication. Appl. Occup. Environ Hygiene 14(9):577-582.

Technical Notes

[1] Laboratories have not used particle counting for crystalline silica analysis for many years. Exposure data is now reported gravimetrically. However, OSHA's construction PEL for crystalline silica, established in 1971, is still listed as a particle-count value. (See Appendix E to OSHA's National Emphasis Program for Crystalline Silica, CPL 03-00-007, for a detailed discussion of the conversion factor used to transform gravimetric measurements to particle-count values). In this guidance, OSHA is using the general industry PEL (0.1 mg/m³ of respirable quartz as an 8-hour time-weighted average) as a benchmark to describe the effectiveness of control measures. The benchmark is approximately equivalent to the general industry silica PEL. Other organizations suggest more stringent levels. For example, the National Institute for Occupational Safety and Health (NIOSH) recommends that respirable crystalline silica exposures be limited to 0.05 mg/m³ as a 10-hour time-weighted average (NIOSH, 2002c). The American Conference of Governmental Industrial Hygienists (ACGIH) recommends that respirable crystalline silica exposures be limited to 0.025 mg/m³ as an 8-hour time-weighted average (ACGIH, 2008).

[2] Among data obtained by OSHA for common construction jobs, tuckpointers' mean and median respirable silica exposures are the highest, with concrete surface grinder operators second highest. Flanagan et al. (2003) found that, at the nine construction sites evaluated, concrete surface grinder operators had the highest average exposure, with tuckpointers next highest. Other groups evaluated included jackhammer operators, rock drillers, concrete saw operators, crusher operators and employees performing cleaning activities at construction sites.

[3] For data compiled by OSHA, the median exposure level for handheld grinder operators exceeded 0.2 mg/m³.

[4] Assuming exposure continued at the same level for the entire shift, as is the case for some grinder operators.

[5] NIOSH (2000a) reported that an employee retrofitted grinding equipment used for tuckpointing. Simcox et al. (1999) reported that several employers retrofit the grinders and polishers their employees used on granite.

[6] Using more water will help keep the slurry thin and unobtrusive, but can result in runoff if not controlled.

[7] Results for the period evaluated were 0.39, 0.78, and 1.2 mg/m³. If no additional exposure had occurred, the associated 8-hour time-weighted average (TWA) would have been 0.16, 0.31, and 0.34 mg/m³ for samples of 191 to 135 minutes duration. However, it is not uncommon for grinder operators to work at the same task for a full shift.

[8] The average of four general area silica levels (0.14, 0.16, 0.16, and 0.27 mg/m³) in the middle of the room was 0.18 mg/m³. As expected, the grinder's exposure was higher (0.66 mg/m³) during the same 3-hour period.

[9] The TWA is calculated by averaging the measured exposure over a specific period of time (in this case a full 8-hour shift).

[10] Consultant provided only an 8-hour TWA result. The construction firm did not continue use of the backpack vacuum because its weight was considered too awkward (for bridge construction work).

[11] The filter was rated as 99.99 percent efficient when tested with respirable-sized particles in accordance with European Standard DIN 24184.

[12] The employee primarily operated the grinder, but performed concrete chipping for a brief period on one day. The result of 0.18 mg/m³ suggests the period of chipping had little impact on his total exposure for the period sampled.

[13] The sample pump worn by the operator faulted; however, a high volume sample in the area indicated airborne concentration of 0.02 mg/m³, the same as the operator's reported exposure level and much lower than results for area samples during uncontrolled grinding. The result associated with the helper was below the limit of detection for the 342-minute sampling period. The grinder was operated for about 80 percent of the time as the employee smoothed walls in a room open to the outdoors on one end and to an atrium on the other. During uncontrolled grinding at the same site, NIOSH obtained a result of 0.66 mg/m³ (grinding 75 percent of the time). During this sampling period, the quick-interrupt electrical circuit breaker cut the power off several times, possibly because water caused an electrical short in this grinder.

[14] These samples of 212 and 431 minutes in duration resulted in 8-hour TWAs of 0.08 and 0.36 mg/m³.

[15] The bulk silica concentration (30 percent) at the first site was lower than at the second site (50 percent). However, the difference in silica content can only account for roughly 40 percent of the large difference between exposure values for the two processes. Results are associated with 8-hour TWA values between 2.4 and 3.8 mg/m³ (if the employees had not had additional exposures) for samples collected over 4 hours.

Tuckpointing/Mortar Removal

This section covers the use of handheld angle grinders for renovation of deteriorating mortar in brick, stone and concrete block buildings (tuckpointing/mortar removal). The term "silica" used in this document refers to respirable crystalline silica.

Introduction

Exposure to fine particles of silica has been shown to cause silicosis, a serious and sometimes fatal lung disease. Construction employees who inhale fine particles of silica may be at risk of developing this disease. Employees who use handheld angle grinders to remove deteriorating mortar between brick, stone and concrete block units generate significant amounts of silica-containing dusts. During this operation, referred to as tuckpointing, small silica particles become suspended in the air and, when inhaled, penetrate deep into employees' lungs. Brick and building renovation masons have been diagnosed with silicosis (Lyons et al., 2007).[1]

Air monitoring shows that typical silica exposure levels for employees using angle grinders without dust collection controls are in excess of the Occupational Safety and Health Administration's (OSHA) benchmark of 0.1 mg/m³ (milligrams of silica per cubic meter of air) as an 8-hour time-weighted average (TWA), an exposure approximately equivalent to OSHA's general industry permissible exposure limit (PEL).[2] In fact, on average, tuckpointers' silica exposures (along with those of surface grinder operators) are among the highest in the construction industry.[3] Among data collected by OSHA, more than half of employee exposures exceed 1.0 mg/m³ during tuckpointing activities, and frequently reach 2.4 mg/m³. Even higher levels are not uncommon (OSHA Case Files).[4]

This document describes methods available to reduce employees' exposures to silica when performing tuckpointing operations.

Although not widely used, vacuum dust collection systems are the most readily available means for controlling silica dust during tuckpointing. With careful work practices, this form of dust control can lower silica exposures substantially. Nevertheless, this method generally will not reduce dust levels below regulatory limits and employers must take additional steps to protect employees. Wet methods are not generally used for tuckpointing because they deposit a slurry of mortar dust and water on the brick, and the water used may penetrate the building envelope.

Grinders who perform tuckpointing without dust controls are frequently exposed to extremely high silica levels. (Photo courtesy of CPWR.)

Silica Dust Control Measures

Vacuum Dust Collection Systems

Vacuum dust collection (VDC) systems for grinders include a shroud, which surrounds the grinding wheel, and a vacuum to pull air through the shroud. Many manufacturers offer grinders with dust collection options. Employers may also purchase equipment to retrofit grinders for vacuum dust collection. The effectiveness of vacuum systems depends on several factors, including the user's technique, the surfaces being finished and the efficiency of the dust collection system.

The addition of the shroud and vacuum hose may make it more difficult to work effectively while reaching above the shoulder, but improved visibility due to reduced dust levels contributes to increased efficiency.

Visible and Respirable Dust
Visible dust contains large particles that are easy to see. The tiny, respirable-sized particles (those that can get into the deep lung) containing silica pose the greatest hazard and are not visible. Most dust-generating construction activities produce a mixture of visible and respirable particles.

Do use visible dust as a general guide for improving dust suppression efforts. If you see visible dust being generated, emissions of respirable silica are probably too high. Measures that control tool-generated dust at the source usually reduce *all* types of particle emissions, including respirable particles.

Do not rely *only* on visible dust to assess the extent of the silica hazard. There may be airborne respirable dust present that is not visible to the naked eye.

Recommendations for Vacuum Dust Collection Systems. The American Conference of Governmental Industrial Hygienists (ACGIH) recommends airflow of 25 cubic feet per minute (CFM) per inch of blade diameter (for example, a 4-inch grinder would need a vacuum with airflow of 100 CFM) (ACGIH, 2007). If airflow is too low, the hose may clog with particulate matter. A study by Croteau et al. (2002), which tested an abrasive wheel saw, indicated that a ventilation flow rate of 75 CFM and an air velocity of 3440 feet per minute (FPM) should be considered the minimum ventilation rate for a 2-inch diameter vacuum hose.

VDC systems can be purchased as a kit. These kits should include a grinder shroud, vacuum, vacuum hose and filter(s). The components of a VDC system are discussed below.

- *Grinder shroud:* Use a shroud appropriate for the grinder and wheel size that provides adequate visibility.

- *Vacuum:* Choose a vacuum with the appropriate power and capacity for your job. A flow rate of 80 CFM or better on a vacuum dust collection system will give the best results while performing mortar removal (Heitbrink and Watkins, 2001).

- *Vacuum hose:* Use the vacuum hose recommended by the manufacturer or that comes with the equipment. Airflow resistance increases with hose length; hoses more than 10 to 15 feet in length should be avoided.

- *Filters:* Double filtration is important. The use of a high-efficiency particulate air (HEPA) filter is critical to prevent the escape of respirable silica dust from the vacuum exhaust. HEPA filters are at least 99.97 percent efficient in removing fine dust particles from the air. A prefilter or cyclonic separator in addition to a HEPA filter will extend the service life of the more costly HEPA filter. A cyclonic separator removes large particles that are capable of overloading or clogging the filter (Heitbrink and Collingwood, 2005).

- *Systematic cleaning:* Choose a vacuum equipped with a back-pulse filter cleaning cycle. Such auto-cleaning mechanisms will reduce the time required for vacuum maintenance and improve the overall efficiency of the dust collection system. If the vacuum does not have an auto-cleaning mechanism, the employee can periodically turn the vacuum cleaner on and off. This allows the bag to collapse and causes the prefilter cake to dislodge from the filter.

- *Monitoring VDC efficiency:* Purchasing a dust collection system equipped with a static pressure gauge allows the employee to monitor the system's efficiency. Systems lacking a static pressure gauge can be monitored visually. If a dust plume increases and becomes more visible where the shroud meets the working surface, the system is not working efficiently (Heitbrink and Collingwood, 2005).

System Maintenance. For optimal dust collection, the following measures are recommended:

- Keep the vacuum hose clear and free of debris, kinks and tight bends. Maintain the vacuum at peak performance to ensure adequate airflow through the shroud and vacuum hoses.

- For vacuums with back-pulse filter cleaning systems, activate the system frequently (several times per day). Empty collection bags and vacuums as frequently as necessary. Dispose of collected dust in a way that prevents it from becoming resuspended in the air.

- For best results, set up a regular schedule for filter cleaning and maintenance. For example, institute a rule to clean the filter or change the bag at each break. This will prevent pressure loss and ensure that exhaust airflow stays more constant on the VDC system.

- Remember, the absence of visible dust does not necessarily mean that employees are adequately protected from silica exposure.

Work Practice Controls to Enhance Vacuum Effectiveness. Studies have shown that the effectiveness of vacuum dust collection systems is enhanced by the use of proper work practices (NIOSH, 1999; Croteau et al., 2002). However, use of these work techniques without a dust collection system will not substantially reduce dust exposures.

- *Blade insertions:* Place the left-hand side of the shroud against the working surface before blade insertion.[5] This directs the dust into the shroud as the blade cuts into the mortar joint.

- *Blade depth:* Per job specification, maintain the full depth of the cut into the mortar. This allows the shroud to remain flush against the working surface and minimizes the dust that escapes from the collection system.

- *One-way movement:* Avoid moving the grinder back and forth along the slot as this will create an open space ahead of the grinder and increase dust escape. For better results, move the grinder in one direction, making a second pass only if necessary.

- *Grinding direction:* Grind counter to the direction of blade rotation to minimize escaping dust.

- *Blade removal:* Backing off the blade a few inches (2 to 4 inches) before removing it from the slot will permit the vacuum to clear accumulated dust.

- *Force:* Use normal (not excessive) force when operating the tool to help keep the leading tool edge flush against the working surface.

Leaving a large gap between the shroud and uncut mortar (see Figure 1a) and not utilizing a high enough airflow exhaust rate will allow dust to escape and may expose employees to high levels of respirable silica (Collingwood and Heitbrink, 2007). Reducing the size of the gap significantly (see Figure 1b) and maintaining a high exhaust airflow rate ensures that most of the dust generated from tuckpointing is captured.

Figure 1. Mortar Removal

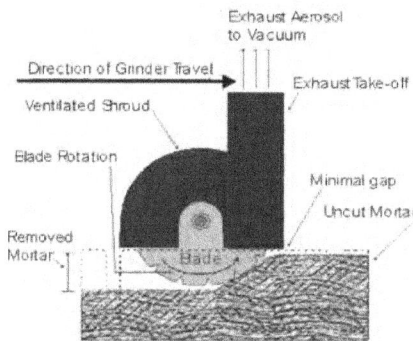

1a. A large gap between the shroud and uncut mortar permits air containing pulverized mortar to escape.

1b. Minimizing the gap between the shroud and uncut mortar allows for good capture of pulverized mortar coming off the blade.

(Illustration courtesy of S. Collingwood and W.A. Heitbrink.)

The following case studies indicate silica exposure levels found under certain uncontrolled conditions, and show the effectiveness of controls in reducing silica exposures.

Uncontrolled Exposures

Case Study I: Several silica samples were collected at two unrelated building renovation sites. Neither group of tuckpointers used dust controls. At the first site, respirable silica exposures for all four employees evaluated were greater than 1.4 mg/m³. Exposure results were even higher at the second location, where all tuckpointer exposure results exceeded 2.4 mg/m³. At both sites, the highest tuckpointer exposures ranged from 7.0 mg/m³ to 8.0 mg/m³ (OSHA Case Files).

Case Study II: A foreman and a mason were evaluated while they performed tuckpointing on a humid day with variable wind. Their respirable silica exposures were between 1.0 mg/m³ and 1.5 mg/m³. These levels exceeded regulatory limits and might have been even higher had it not been for the windy and humid weather conditions (OSHA Case File).[7]

Controlled Exposures

Case Study III: NIOSH collected 13 respirable silica samples for tuckpointers using angle-grinders equipped with a VDC system consisting of a shroud, hose and vacuum. Although exposures were less than those uncontrolled exposures previously discussed, more than half of the employees had exposures above 0.5 mg/m³ (NIOSH, 1999).

Case Study IV: A study showed the benefits of using dust controls by comparing tuckpointers' exposures with and without the use of vacuum dust collection equipment. The dust collection system consisted of a shroud on the grinder and a hose attachment leading to a dust collection bag. Initial tests showed that silica exposures with controls were 37 to 47 percent lower than when controls were not used, even though employees had difficulty using the shroud properly. Subsequently, the manufacturer adjusted the shroud and rearranged the handle and hose attachment to make the equipment easier to handle. In a follow-up test, the modified equipment reduced the employees' respirable silica exposure by 93 percent, from 4.0 mg/m³ (uncontrolled) to 0.3 mg/m³. While this reduction is significant, the authors concluded that respiratory protection is still required in order to provide employees using dust collection equipment with adequate protection (Nash and Williams, 2000).[8]

Case Study V: Wet methods are not commonly used for tuckpointing because they may deposit a slurry consisting of mortar dust and water on the brick. The applied water may also penetrate the structure and damage the interior. However, in some cases, wet methods can be used in tuckpointing operations. For example, in this case study, an employee modified a tuckpointing grinder with both a ventilation shroud and a small water application nozzle. During one hour of mortar grinding, the employee's respirable dust exposure (0.38 mg/m³) was less than 3 percent of the median value for five results obtained for uncontrolled mortar grinding in this study (13.3 mg/m³) (NIOSH, 2000).

In this case study, the employee used a hand-pump garden sprayer to pressurize the water, which was applied to the blade at a rate slightly less than a quart per minute through a nozzle made of 1/16-inch copper tubing. A wet/dry shop vacuum connected to the shroud removed the damp mortar debris as it was generated. A 10-foot vacuum hose extension (PVC pipe) allowed the employee to stand an extra 10 feet away from the vacuum for added protection from dust escaping from the vacuum.

This study was performed using an electric grinder, which introduces electrical safety issues because it is an electric tool being used in a wet environment. One way to avoid possible electrical safety issues related to the introduction of water is to switch to a pneumatic grinder (NIOSH, 2000).

Compressed Air
The use of compressed air to clean surfaces or clothing is strongly discouraged. Using compressed air to clean work surfaces or clothing can significantly increase employee exposure, especially in enclosed and semi-enclosed spaces. Cleaning should be performed with a HEPA-filtered vacuum or by wet methods.

Respiratory Protection and Engineering Control Evaluation

It is not uncommon for respirable crystalline silica exposures to reach 2.4 mg/m³ or higher while tuckpointing without engineering controls. Tuckpointing is often conducted in situations or on materials that do not permit the use of wet methods as an engineering control.

In these situations, VDC systems are recommended. A VDC system attached to the angle grinder will lower silica exposures; however, since exposures may still exceed 0.1 mg/m³ with controls, respiratory protection will be required to supplement the VDC system. When working in an open or semi-enclosed area with a properly functioning VDC system, the employee may be able to wear a properly fitted, NIOSH-approved half-facepiece or disposable respirator equipped with an N-, R- or P-95 filter.

In any workplace where respirators are necessary to protect the health of the employee, or whenever respirators are required by the employer, the employer must establish and implement a written respiratory protection program with worksite-specific procedures and elements. These should include the selection of respirators, medical evaluations of employees, fit testing, proper usage, maintenance and care, cleaning and disinfecting, proper air quality/quantity and training (see 29 CFR 1926.103).

When tuckpointing in enclosed areas or when environmental conditions, such as wind, concentrate mortar particles in an employee's breathing zone, exposures may exceed 1.0 mg/m³ even with effective controls. When working in enclosed areas, the employer should supplement the VDC system by providing a properly fitted NIOSH-approved full-facepiece respirator with an N-, R- or P-95 filter. A powered air-purifying respirator (PAPR) offers alternative protection for those who cannot wear a full-facepiece air-purifying respirator. Such respiratory protection is effective for exposures to silica up to 5 mg/m³ for a full-facepiece respirator and up to 10 mg/m³ for a PAPR with a fitted facepiece.

Construction sites often involve many operations occurring simultaneously that can generate respirable silica dust. Therefore, it is important and necessary to utilize effective controls (such as wet methods and/or a VDC system) in order to minimize total exposures to silica-exposed tool operators or potential exposures to other employees.

Since tuckpointing even under controlled conditions can result in silica exposures in excess of 0.1 mg/m³, adjacent employees may need to wear respirators as well. The level of respiratory protection is dependent on the employee's silica exposure, which varies depending on factors in the work environment (such as enclosed, semi-enclosed, or open spaces and/or multiple operations generating silica dust), environmental conditions (such as wind direction and speed), and the percentage of silica found in the material.

Employers should conduct exposure monitoring periodically while controls are being used to ensure that the controls are working properly and that the appropriate level of respiratory protection is being used.

For more information on how to determine proper respiratory protection, visit OSHA's Web site at www.osha.gov. NIOSH's Web site also provides information on respirators at www.cdc.gov/niosh.

References

ACGIH. 2007. Industrial Ventilation, A Manual of Recommended Practice, 26th Edition. American Conference of Governmental Industrial Hygienists, Cincinnati, OH.

ACGIH. 2008. Threshold limit values for chemical substances and physical agents and biological exposure indices. American Conference of Governmental Industrial Hygienists, Cincinnati, OH.

Collingwood, S. and Heitbrink, W.A. 2007. Field evaluation of an engineering control for respirable crystalline silca exposures during mortar removal. J Occup Environ Hygiene 4:875-887.

Croteau, G.A., Guffey, S.E., Flanagan, M.E. and Seixas, N.S. 2002. The effects of local exhaust ventilation controls on dust exposures during concrete cutting and grinding activities. Am Ind Hygiene Assoc J 63(4): 458-467.

Flanagan, M.E., Seixas, N., Majar, M., Camp, J. and Morgan, M. 2003. Silica dust exposures during selected construction activities. Am Ind Hygiene Assn J 64(3):319-28. May-June, 2003.

Heitbrink, W.A. and Watkins, D.S. 2001. The effect of exhaust flow rate upon the respirable dust emissions for tuckpointing operations. In: In-Depth Study Report: Control Technology for Crystalline Silica Exposures in Construction. U.S. Department of Health and Human Services, Centers for Disease Control and Prevention, National Institute for Occupational Safety and Health. ECTB No. 247-18.

Heitbrink, W. and Collingwood, S. 2005. Protecting Tuckpointing Workers from Silica Dust: Draft Recommendations for Ventilated Grinder. The Center to Protect Workers' Rights (CPWR). www.cpwr.com

Lyons, J.J., Sime, P.J., Ward, D., Watson, T., Abraham, J.L., Evans, R., Budev, M., Costas, K. and Beckett, W.S. 2007. A breathless builder. Breathe 3:386-390.

Nash, N.T. and Williams, D.R. 2000. Occupational exposure to crystalline silica during tuckpointing and the use of engineering controls. Appl Occup Environ Hygiene 15(1):8-10. January, 2000.

NIOSH. 1996. Preventing silicosis and deaths in construction workers. Dept. of Health and Human Services, National Institute for Occupational Safety and Health. Publication No. 96-112.

NIOSH, 1998. Environmental surveillance report: Construction site #16, Covington, KY. National Institute for Occupational Safety and Health, Morgantown, WV. June, 1998.

NIOSH. 1999. Control technology and exposure assessment for occupational exposure to crystalline silica: Case 23—Masonry Tuckpointing (ECTB 233-123c). National Institute for Occupational Safety and Health, Cincinnati, OH.

NIOSH, 2000. In-depth survey report: Control technology for crystalline silica exposures in construction: Exposures and preliminary control evaluation at various sites for Bricklayers Local #9, Pittsburgh, Pennsylvania (ECTB 247-12). National Institute for Occupational Safety and Health, Cincinnati, OH. February, 2000.

NIOSH. 2002. Pocket guide to chemical hazards. Pub. No. 2002-140. National Institute for Occupational Safety and Health, Cincinnati, OH. June, 2002.

OSHA. 1996. Ground-fault protection on construction sites. Occupational Safety and Health Administration, Office of Training and Education. May, 1996.

OSHA Case Files (Special Emphasis Program Inspection Reports from 1996-1998).

Shields, C. 1999. Silica dust exposures from OSHA construction inspections in the Chicago area 1996-1998. Occupational Safety and Health Administration. Aurora, IL, Area Office. Slide Presentation.

Zalk, D. 2002. Personal communication between D. Zalk, Lawrence Livermore Laboratory, CA. and W. Long, Eastern Research Group, Inc., Arlington, VA. October 29, 2002.

Technical Notes

[1] These employees performed a variety of activities involving silica-containing materials, including abrasive blasting and work with fire brick (NIOSH, 1996).

[2] Laboratories have not used particle counting for crystalline silica analysis for many years. Exposure data is now reported gravimetrically. However, OSHA's construction PEL for crystalline silica, established in 1971, is still listed as a particle-count value. (See Appendix E to OSHA's National

Emphasis Program for Crystalline Silica, CPL 03-00-007, for a detailed discussion of the conversion factor used to transform gravimetric measurements to particle-count values). In this guidance, OSHA is using 0.1 mg/m³ of respirable quartz as an 8-hour time-weighted average as a benchmark to describe the effectiveness of control measures. The benchmark is approximately equivalent to the general industry silica PEL. Other organizations suggest more stringent levels. For example, the National Institute for Occupational Safety and Health (NIOSH) recommends that respirable crystalline silica exposures be limited to 0.05 mg/m³ as a 10-hour time-weighted average (NIOSH, 2002). The American Conference of Governmental Industrial Hygienists (ACGIH) recommends that respirable crystalline silica exposures be limited to 0.025 mg/m³ as an 8-hour time-weighted average (ACGIH, 2008).

[3] Among data obtained by OSHA for common construction jobs, tuckpointers' mean and median respirable silica exposures are the highest, with concrete surface grinder operators the second highest. Flanagan et al. (2003) found that, at nine construction sites evaluated, concrete surface grinder operators had the highest average exposure, with tuckpointers next highest. Other groups evaluated included jackhammer operators, rock drillers, concrete saw operators, crusher operators, and employees performing cleaning activities at construction sites.

[4] Among data obtained by OSHA, more than half of employee exposures exceeded 1.0 mg/m³ during tuckpointing and the average exposure level was 2.2 mg/m³. Due to the high levels of dust, many of the samples were collected for a period less than a full shift. However, tuckpointers often work at this task 8 hours per day. Thus, a similar level of exposure is assumed for the unsampled portion of the shift. Even if employees had no further silica exposure beyond the period sampled, the median 8-hour time-weighted average crystalline silica result would exceed 0.5 mg/m³ and the average level would be 1.5 mg/m³.

[5] Assumes typical counter-clockwise blade rotation (or whatever blade direction ensures that the dust will be captured within the shroud).

[6] Results from the two sites include 6 full and 2 partial shift samples. Employees at both sites indicated they typically performed tuckpointing 8 hours per day. Bulk samples showed that the mortar contained 20 to 40 percent silica at the first site and 30 percent silica at the second site (OSHA Case Files).

[7] Bulk samples associated with these results indicate that the mortar contained 50 to 70 percent silica (OSHA Case File).

[8] Initially, employees at two sites were monitored for 5 to 7 hours each; in the follow-up test, sample times were 1 to 2 hours. All results were reported as 8-hour time-weighted averages. In the final test, the respirable silica exposure without dust controls was 4.08 mg/m³, compared to 0.31 mg/m³ with the modified dust collection system (Nash and Williams, 2000).

Jackhammers

This section covers breaker hammers (jackhammers) used in the breaking and demolition of concrete, asphalt and other materials. The term "silica" used in this document refers to respirable crystalline silica.

Introduction

Exposure to fine particles of silica has been shown to cause silicosis, a serious and sometimes fatal lung disease. Construction employees who inhale fine particles of silica may be at risk of developing this disease. Employees produce dusts containing silica when they use breaker hammers (commonly known as jackhammers) to chip and break rocks or concrete. The hammer's crushing action generates small particles that easily become suspended in the air and, when inhaled, penetrate deep into employees' lungs.

The Occupational Safety and Health Administration (OSHA) compiled exposure monitoring results for construction workers using jackhammers outdoors without dust suppression. Employee exposures frequently exceeded OSHA's benchmark of 0.1 mg/m³ (milligrams of silica per cubic meter of air) as an 8-hour time-weighted average (TWA), an exposure approximately equivalent to OSHA's general industry permissible exposure limit (PEL) for construction.[1] The results showed operator exposures that reached 0.8 mg/m³ during the period evaluated. More than one-third of the jackhammer operators experienced exposures between 0.1 mg/m³ and 0.5 mg/m³.[2] When breaking concrete indoors, operator exposure levels were 3.0 mg/m³ or higher (NIOSH, 1983). Another set of exposure monitoring results showed 178 jackhammer and chipping gun samples with a mean silica exposure of 0.15 mg/m³ (Flanagan et al., 2006).

This section discusses methods for reducing silica exposures among construction workers using jackhammers. The principle means to control silica dust from jackhammer operations is by wetting the dust at the point of breaking or chipping (i.e., wet methods). In comparison, an experiment was conducted testing the efficiency of dust collection on a jackhammer. In the study, the jackhammer was retrofitted with a commercially available rock drill shroud connected to a vacuum dust collection system. The results of the study showed that the dust collection system reduced respirable dust exposures by almost 60 percent (Echt et al., 2003).

Employee chipping concrete with a jackhammer while using a wet method. (Photo courtesy of NIOSH.)

Silica Dust Control Measures

Wet Methods

Wet methods reduce dust by wetting the material at the impact point, before the dust gets into the air. Wet particles are heavier and more likely to stick to each other than dry particles and tend to settle more quickly. Thus, wet methods decrease the amount of particulate matter suspended in the air. This form of dust suppression is effective for both respirable and visible dust.

The ideal wet method of dust control uses the minimum amount of water to get the maximum result. Spray directed at the point of impact is optimal. The spray must not be too fine otherwise the air motion around the jackhammer will not allow the spray to contact dust at the impact point. For example, employees operating 90-pound jackhammers reduced their silica exposure between 50 and 98 percent using just ⅛ gallon of water per minute as a spray (Zalk, 2002).

Water for dust suppression can be applied manually, or using a semi-automated water-feed device.

Manual spraying

In the simplest method for suppressing dust, a dedicated helper directs a constant spray of water at the impact point, while another employee operates the jackhammer. The helper can use a hose with a garden-style nozzle to maintain a steady and carefully directed spray at the impact point where material is broken and crushed.

An experienced helper will be able to adjust the water flow to achieve the maximum dust suppression using the minimum amount of water, thus reducing water run-off.

Periodically picking up a hose and spraying the general area is not effective. Simply pre-wetting the concrete or asphalt prior to breaking the surface is also ineffective (see Case Studies II and III, at Page 35). Because the jackhammer continues to break through silica-containing material, dust is constantly produced. To be effective, spray application must be continuous and directed at the point of impact.

Water Spray System

This alternative uses the same principle as manual spraying, but eliminates the need for a helper to hold the hose.

Jackhammers retrofitted with a spray nozzle aimed at the tip of the tool offer a dramatic decrease in silica exposure. Although water-fed jackhammers are not commercially available, it is neither expensive nor difficult to retrofit equipment and parts are available at well-stocked hardware stores (Zalk, 2000, 2001, 2002).

Visible and Respirable Dust

Visible dust contains large particles that are easy to see. The tiny, respirable-sized particles (those that can get into the deep lung) containing silica pose the greatest hazard and are not visible. Most dust-generating construction activities produce a mixture of visible and respirable particles.

Do use visible dust as a general guide for improving dust suppression efforts. If you see visible dust being generated, emissions of respirable silica are probably too high. Measures that control tool-generated dust at the source usually reduce *all* types of particle emissions, including respirable particles.

Do not rely *only* on visible dust to assess the extent of the silica hazard. There may be airborne respirable dust present that is not visible to the naked eye.

Designing a water spray dust control system for a jackhammer. Employers can design their own wet method dust control system (NIOSH, 2008). The system requires:

- A **water source** (e.g., a municipal tap, a tank truck); a **valve** to control water flow from the source (if the source does not have its own flow control valve); and a **hose** or tubing to bring water from the source to the jackhammer.

- Additional **flexible, but durable, tubing** to supply water along the jackhammer to the nozzle.[3]

- A sturdy water **flow control valve** mounted on the jackhammer to make minor adjustments in the flow. A water flow rate of 350 ml/min (0.09 gallons/min) in conjunction with a spray angle of 80 degrees (the angle included between the sides of the cone formed by the water discharged from the nozzle) is recommended recommended for achieving optimal reductions in silica exposure.

- A good-quality garden-style **spray nozzle**, which can can provide either a spray or stream of water.

- ***Fittings*** to connect the hose, valves and tubing, and to mount the nozzle to the hammer body.

NIOSH has prepared a web-based practical engineering pamphlet on the use of water spray controls for jackhammers (NIOSH, 2008).

Using multiple jackhammers without dust controls increases silica exposures for both operators and adjacent employees. (Photo courtesy of Kenneth Linch.)

System Maintenance. Routine maintenance helps ensure that the equipment functions as intended. Considerations include:

Clogged nozzles: Dust and debris can clog spray nozzles. Check the nozzle frequently, especially if the job starts looking dusty. Activate the spray for a few seconds and observe the spray to be sure the water flow is appropriate and directed at the tool tip. The nozzle should be cleaned or changed if it is dripping, spitting, squirting, or spraying at an odd angle. Keep spare nozzles on hand for quick changes at the worksite.

Spray angle: The spray nozzle position is critical. Check the water spray angle frequently.
- Is the spray focused on the breakpoint?
- Is the spray wetting the dust before it can disperse from the tip of the hammer?

Consistent water flow: Take steps to provide consistent water flow. Prevent interruptions from kinked hoses, vehicular traffic running over hoses and large drops in water pressure. Ensure an adequate supply of water.

Using a Water-Fed Jackhammer

Make sure that the water spray covers the tip of the tool blade.

Adjust water flow as often as necessary. A water flow rate of about 350 ml/min (0.09 gallons/min) is optimal in most circumstances. Many factors affect the exact water requirement. Water flow onto the impact point is an important element in reducing silica exposure to the operator. However, the angle of water delivery is just as important. A coned-shape spray angle of 80 degrees is recommended. This will provide the greatest reduction in silica exposure to the operator. (Echt et al., 2003; Zalk, 2002; WorkSafe Western Australia, 1996). More water is usually not better.

As a rule of thumb, try to adjust the nozzle and water flow to prevent visible dust release.

Employees may wish to keep a damp cloth handy to wipe their protective faceshields or eyewear.

Freezing Temperatures. Freezing temperatures complicate the use of water. Consider heating the local work area, if practical, to prevent ice from forming in the water-feed system. Large portable heating units are commonly used to heat commercial and sometimes road and highway projects. Drain the system when not in use. If water freezes on the ground, chip away the ice or use deicing compounds or sand to control the slipping hazard.

Enclosed Areas. A study of wet methods showed that they work as well indoors as outdoors for jackhammers (Zalk, 2000). However, the decreased airflow in enclosed areas can increase dust concentrations. Provide good fresh air circulation as an extra level of protection for jackhammer operators working indoors or inside containments as concentrations can increase quickly if controls are not functioning optimally.

Water runoff. Comply with local requirements for managing the used water. If a considerable runoff is generated, it may be necessary to channel the water to a point where it can be collected for treatment.[4]

Case Studies

The following case studies indicate silica exposure levels found under certain uncontrolled or poorly controlled conditions, and show the effectiveness of controls in reducing silica exposures.

Uncontrolled

Case Study I: Five jackhammer operators chipping damaged sections of a concrete bridge deck for an entire shift had silica exposures between 0.2 and 0.5 mg/m³. A sixth operator's exposure was 0.09 mg/m³. In the same area, laborers' exposures also ranged between 0.2 and 0.5 mg/m³. The use of compressed air to blow chips out of cracks may have contributed to their exposures (Shields, 2000a). Results fell in this range at nearly half of the construction sites for which OSHA compiled data.[5]

How Reliable are Wet Methods for Controlling Respirable Silica Dust?

Wet methods are only as reliable as their application. If you can answer "Yes" to the following questions, the dust control is probably working well.

- Is there enough water and water pressure to create a spray?
- Is the spray directed to envelop the area where dust is released – at the tip of the tool?
- Does the operator make adjustments as needed to ensure that water spray is constantly applied to the correct area?
- Is visible dust suppressed?[6]

Improper Use of Water to Control Dust

Case Study II: Employees at an indoor construction site wet the surface before (but not *during*) jackhammer use. Their silica exposures were about 0.2 mg/m³ (OSHA Case File).

Case Study III: At a second indoor site, exposures of more than 0.6 mg/m³ were reported for two employees who *inconsistently* sprayed water while operating jackhammers. These results significantly exceed OSHA limits. A small fan in the window was inadequate to blow contaminated air out of the space and a cooling fan aimed at the employees simply recirculated the dust (OSHA Case File).

Effective Wet Methods

Case Study IV: A construction employee was using a jackhammer to break concrete on a bridge next to a freeway while another employee continuously aimed a water hose at the breaking point. No silica was detected in the first employee's breathing area over a 6-hour period. Air sampling results were well below 0.1 mg/m³ (OSHA Case File).[7]

Case Study V: In an water spray to the impact point. With dust control in place, exposure levels of less than or equal to 0.1 mg/m³ were found both indoors and outdoors (Zalk, 2000).

Air monitoring was conducted to measure silica exposure levels while the employees operated the equipment dry (no water flow). Additional monitoring was performed with the water turned on and adjusted to carefully apply spray to the break point. The experiment was repeated indoors, with the employees breaking concrete in a shed on the same parking lot, first using dry equipment, then with the water on.[8]

Using dry methods, the employee exposure levels for silica were 0.2 to 0.8 mg/m³ outdoors and approximately 0.9 to nearly 4.3 mg/m³ indoors. The outdoor experimental results were within the range observed for employees on construction sites operating jackhammers for the full shift. The indoor results were somewhat higher than reported in compiled OSHA samples.[9]

In this study, employee exposures dropped dramatically when dust was controlled by applying water spray to the impact point. With dust control in place, exposure levels of less than or equal to 0.1 mg/m³ were found both indoors and outdoors (Zalk, 2000).

Case Study VI: In this study, Echt et al., (2003) evaluated the effectiveness of vacuum dust collection (VDC) and water-spray controls attached to a jackhammer. The water-spray control was very effective in reducing respirable dust concentrations compared to the VDC control. The water-spray attachment delivered approximately 350 milliliters (ml) of water per minute (0.09 gallons/min). This water flow rate did not add a substantial amount of water to the work surface.

Water spray controls that use commercially available nozzles offer variable reduction in exposures based on flow rate and spray angle. A reduction in exposure to silica of approximately 40 percent was achieved using a flow rate of 250 ml/min (0.07 gallons/min) at a spray angle of 60 degrees. However, the reduction in exposure was increased to around 70 percent with an increased flow rate at 300 ml/min (0.08 gallons/min) and a spray angle of 80 degrees (Echt et al., 2004).

Case Study VII: Brouwer et al., (2004) conducted a study which investigated the effectiveness of water

application while using jackhammers and plate compactors. Two types of jackhammers were analyzed in the study, heavy and light. The study involved breaking concrete slabs in an inside area of approximately 145,000 cubic feet with the heavy jackhammer and breaking concrete floor tile with a light jackhammer in a small enclosed bathroom area of approximately 160 cubic feet. The water flow rate on the light jackhammer was 190 ml/min, while the flow rate was 170 ml/min for the heavy jackhammer. Both jackhammers operated at 5 bar pressure. The water holding tank, a backpack, held a total of 15 liters.

Results of the silica exposure were calculated as task-based time-weighted average concentrations. Silica concentrations for the light jackhammer without the use of water ranged from 0.12 to 1.75 mg/m³ compared to the use of wet methods, which resulted in exposures ranging from 0.04 to 0.67 mg/m³. Results of the heavy jackhammer without controls were 0.08 to 0.66 mg/m³. Exposure results after wet methods were employed ranged from 0.02 to 0.36 mg/m³ respirable silica. (Brouwer et al., 2004).

Compressed Air

The use of compressed air to clean surfaces or clothing is strongly discouraged. Using compressed air to clean work surfaces or clothing can significantly increase employee exposure, especially in enclosed and semi-enclosed spaces. Cleaning should be performed with a HEPA-filtered vacuum or by wet methods.

Respiratory Protection and Engineering Control Evaluation

Jackhammering without engineering controls or using engineering controls in an ineffective manner (for example, trickling water at the point of impact), can cause exposures to respirable crystalline silica that exceed 3.0 mg/m³.

Selection and use of respiratory protection is based on exposure, which is primarily affected by four factors: Use of effective wet methods; length of time jackhammers are in operation; indoor versus outdoor operations; and number of jackhammers in operation at a given time.

Effective wet methods provide the best option for reducing silica exposures. Data show that outdoor jackhammering using effective wet methods for operations under four hours duration will control exposures below 0.1 mg/m³. Under such circumstances, operators may not be required to wear respiratory protection.

Because exposures can exceed 0.1 mg/m^3, but remain below 1.0 mg/m^3, it may be necessary to use a properly fitted, NIOSH-approved half-face-piece or disposable air purifying respirator equipped with an N-, R- or P-95 filter under the following conditions:

• When operating a jackhammer outdoors with effective wet methods for more than four hours.

• When operating multiple jackhammers outdoors outdoors in close proximity (i.e., within 15 feet) with effective wet methods for less than four hours.

• When operating a single jackhammer in enclosed spaces or indoors with effective wet methods.

Because exposures can exceed 1.0 mg/m^3, it may be necessary to use a properly fitted, NIOSH-approved full-facepiece air purifying respirator equipped with an N-, R- or P-95 filter under the following conditions:

• When operating multiple jackhammers indoors while using effective wet methods.

• In situations where wet methods are not feasible during any operation of two or more jackhammers.

In any workplace where respirators are necessary to protect the health of the employee, or whenever respirators are required by the employer, the employer must establish and implement a written respiratory protection program with worksite-specific procedures and elements. These should include the selection of respirators, medical evaluations of employees, fit testing, proper usage, maintenance and care, cleaning and disinfecting, proper air quality/quantity and training (see 29 CFR 1926.103).

Other employees in close proximity to the work operations where silica dust is generated may also need respiratory protection if effective controls are not implemented. The level of protection is dependent on the employee's silica exposure, which varies depending on factors in the work environment (such as enclosed, semi-enclosed, or open spaces and/or multiple operations generating silica dust), environmental conditions (such as wind direction and speed), and the percentage of silica found in the material.

Construction sites often involve many operations occurring simultaneously that can generate respirable silica dust. Therefore, it is important and necessary to utilize effective controls (such as wet methods) in order to minimize total exposures to silica-exposed tool operators or potential exposures to other employees.

Employers should conduct exposure monitoring periodically while controls are being used to ensure that the controls are working properly and that the appropriate level of respiratory protection is being used.

For more information on how to determine proper respiratory protection, visit OSHA's Web site at www.osha.gov. NIOSH's Web site also provides information on respirators at www.cdc.gov/niosh.

References

ACGIH. 2001. Threshold limit values for chemical substances and physical agents and biological exposure indices. American Conference of Governmental Industrial Hygienists, Cincinnati, OH.

Brouwer, D.H., Spee, T., Huijbers, R.F., Lurvink, M.W.M., Fritjers, A.C.P. 2004. Effectiveness of dust control by atomisation of water sprays on handheld demolition and soil compacting equipment. Tijdschrift voor toegepaste Arbowetenschap 4:68-74, 2004.

Croteau, G.A., Guffey, S.E, Flanagan, M.E. and Seixas, N.S. 2002. The effects of local exhaust ventilation controls on dust exposures during concrete cutting and grinding activities. Am Ind Hygiene Assoc. J 63(4): 458-467, 2002.

Echt, A., Sieber, K., Jones, E., Schill, D., Lefkowitz, D., Sugar, J., Hoffner, K. 2003. Control respirable dust and crystalline silica from breaking concrete with a jackhammer. Appl Occup Environ Hygiene 18(7): 491-495, 2003.

Echt, A., Sieber, K., Williams, D., Cantrell, A., Schill, D.P., Lefkowitz, D., Sugar, J., Hoffner, K. 2004. In-depth survey report of a water spray device for suppressing respirable and crystalline silica dust from jackhammers at E.E. Cruz Co.. South Plainfield, NJ. Cincinnati, OH: U.S. Department of Health and Human Services, Centers for Disease Control and Prevention, National Institute for Occupational Safety and Health, Report No. EPHB 282-11c2.

Flanagan, M.E., Seixas, N., Becker, P., Takacs, B., Camp, J. 2006. Silica exposure on construction sites: results of an exposure monitoring data compilation project. J Occup Environ Hygiene. 3(3):144-52.

NIOSH. 1983. Health hazard evaluation report: Grand Gulf Nuclear Power Plant, Gibson, Mississippi. HETA 83-132-1508. U.S. Dept. of Health and Human Services, National Institute for Occupational Safety and Health.

NIOSH. 1996. Preventing silicosis and deaths in construction workers. U.S. Dept. of Health and Human Services, National Institute for Occupational Safety and Health, Publication No. 96-112.

NIOSH. 2002. Pocket guide to chemical hazards. Pub. No. 2002-140. National Institute for Occupational Safety and Health, Cincinnati, OH. June, 2002.

NIOSH. 2008. Water Spray Control of Hazardous Dust When Breaking Concrete with a Jackhammer. May, 2008. http://www.cdc.gov/niosh/docs/wp-solutions/ 2008-127.

OSHA. 1996. Ground-fault protection on construction sites. Occupational Safety and Health Administration, Office of Training and Education. May, 1996.

OSHA Case Files (Special Emphasis Program Inspection Reports, 1996-1998).

Shields, C. 2000a. Database: Silica dust exposures associated with construction activities. Occupational Safety and Health Administration, North Aurora, IL. September 14, 2000.

Shields, C. 2000b. Silica dust exposures from OSHA construction inspections in the Chicago area 1996-1999. Occupational Safety and Health Administration, Aurora, IL, Area Office Slide Presentation.

WorkSafe Western Australia. 1996. Silica dust on construction sites. www.wt.com/au/safetyline/ d_pubs/silica.htm. March, accessed 04/15/97.

Zalk, D. 2000. Presentation at the American Industrial Hygiene Conference and Exposition, Orlando, FL. May 24, 2000.

Zalk, D. 2001. Personal communication between D. Zalk, Lawrence Livermore Laboratory, CA, and W. Long and A. Gandhi, Eastern Research Group, Inc., Arlington, VA. January 23, 2001.

Zalk, D. 2002. Personal communication between D. Zalk, Lawrence Livermore Laboratory, CA. and W. Long, Eastern Research Group, Inc., Arlington, VA. October 29, 2002.

Technical Notes

[1] Laboratories have not used particle counting for crystalline silica analysis in many years and now report exposure data gravimetrically. However, OSHA's construction PEL for crystalline silica, established in 1971, is still listed as a particle-count value. (See Appendix E to OSHA's National Emphasis Program for Crystalline Silica, CPL 03-00-007, for a detailed discussion of the conversion factor used to transform gravimetric measurements to particle-count values). In this guidance, OSHA is using 0.1 mg/m^3 of respirable quartz as an 8-hour time-weighted average as a benchmark to describe the effectiveness of control measures. The benchmark is approximately equivalent to the general industry silica PEL. Other organizations suggest more stringent levels. For example, the National Institute for Occupational Safety and Health (NIOSH) recommends that respirable crystalline silica exposures be limited to 0.05 mg/m^3 as a 10-hour time-weighted average (NIOSH, 2002). The American Conference of Governmental Industrial Hygienists (ACGIH) recommends that respirable crystalline silica exposures be limited to 0.025 mg/m^3 as an 8-hour time-weighted average (ACGIH, 2008).

[2] References: OSHA Case Files; Shields, 2000a [data of 3/29, 5/1, 5/11, 7/8, 8/13, and 10/1/99].

[3] Copper tubing, heavy rubber, plastic tubing, and even hydraulic line have been used. The more flexible the tubing, the easier it is to adjust the nozzle position when installing the system.

[4] Under many conditions, 1/8 gallon per minute water flow will generate little run-off. Requirements, however, vary greatly by location. Contact the municipal environmental quality department or other appropriate authority to see if there are any local requirements.

[5] OSHA Case Files; Shields, 2000a [data of 8/13].

[6] Although visible dust cannot be used to predict the amount of respirable-sized dust in the air, if the spray is not controlling the visible dust, it is probably not controlling respirable dust either.

[7] Based on the limit of detection, the employee's respirable silica exposure was calculated to be less than or equal to 0.037 mg/m^3.

[8] All sample durations were 1 to 3 hours.

[9] This level is higher than typical on indoor construction sites, probably because the enclosed shed used in the test was smaller and had less natural ventilation than the indoor spaces evaluated for OSHA's data (primarily parking garages).

Rotary Hammers and Similar Tools

This section covers use of rotary hammers and similar tools to drill small diameter holes in concrete and other masonry construction materials. The term "silica" used in this document refers to respirable crystalline silica.

Introduction

Exposure to fine particles of silica has been shown to cause silicosis, a serious and sometimes fatal lung disease. Construction employees who inhale fine particles of silica may be at risk of developing this disease. Employees produce dusts containing silica when they cut, grind, crush, or drill construction materials such as concrete, masonry, tile, and rock. The small particles easily become suspended in the air and, when inhaled, penetrate deep into employees' lungs.

Using rotary hammers or similar tools to drill small-diameter holes in concrete, bricks, masonry blocks, tiles and similar materials can expose employees to hazardous levels of airborne silica if measures are not taken to suppress dust emissions. At worksites without dust control, data compiled by the Occupational Safety and Health Administration (OSHA) show that employee silica exposures during this type of drilling can exceed the benchmark of 0.1 mg/m³ (milligrams per cubic meter of air) as an 8-hour time-weighted average (TWA), an exposure approximately equivalent to OSHA's general industry permissible exposure limit (PEL) by more than three times (Lofgren, 1993).[1,2] During periods of active drilling, exposures can be as high as 0.78 mg/m³ (NIOSH, 1996).[3]

This section describes methods available to reduce employees' exposures to silica during drilling of concrete and other silica-containing materials. Three primary methods exist to control silica dust while using rotary hammers: (1) vacuum dust collection, (2) dust barriers or enclosures, and (3) wet methods. Each of these methods is easy to implement.

Vacuum dust collection methods can significantly reduce dust emissions during small-diameter hole drilling operations. *Dust barriers* are helpful for employees who drill holes only occasionally. *Wet methods* are generally effective in reducing employee exposures to silica dust and maintaining exposures below OSHA's limits, but are not appropriate with all tools.

Visible and Respirable Dust

Visible dust contains large particles that are easy to see. The tiny, respirable-sized particles (those that can get into the deep lung) containing silica pose the greatest hazard and are not visible. Most dust-generating construction activities produce a mixture of visible and respirable particles.

Do use visible dust as a general guide for improving dust suppression efforts. If you see visible dust being generated, emissions of respirable silica are probably too high. Measures that control tool-generated dust at the source usually reduce *all* types of particle emissions, including respirable particles.

Do not rely *only* on visible dust to assess the extent of the silica hazard. There may be airborne respirable dust present that is not visible to the naked eye.

Silica Dust Control Measures

Vacuum Dust Collection Systems

Vacuum dust collection (VDC) systems are commercially available for handheld drills, usually as add-on systems. The systems enclose the drill bit in a suction ring (dust entrance), which includes a port for attaching a vacuum to collect dust and concrete particles generated during drilling.

Built-in Dust Collection Systems

Some tools that have built-in dust collection systems also use a suction ring and include an integral impeller (rotor blade) that draws dust into a bag or receptacle attached to the drill body.

Built-in dust collection systems are convenient because they require no additional equipment, such as vacuums. However, built-in systems may not provide the same level of employee protection as vacuum systems. Fine particles may pass through the lower-efficiency filter bags or receptacles often used for built-in systems. Also, built-in systems release the exhaust air (and any particles that escape the filter) near the employee's face, while vacuums are typically positioned several feet away.

Recommendations for Vacuum Dust Collection Systems. VDC systems can be purchased as a kit. These kits should include a dust collection device, vacuum, vacuum hose and filter(s). The components of a VDC system are discussed below.

- *Dust Collection Device:* In most cases, this is a retrofit on the rotary hammer; therefore, be sure to follow the manufacturers' directions on installing the dust collector.

- *Vacuum:* Choose a vacuum with the appropriate power and capacity for your job. Obtaining a flow rate on a vacuum dust collection system of 80 cubic feet per minute (CFM) or better will give the best results with a variety of common tools (Heitbrink and Watkins, 2001). In some circumstances, a lower flow rate may be sufficient. Sheperd et al. (2009) found that for small hammer drills a flow rate of 49 CFM was sufficient to capture more than 90 percent of the respirable silica dust generated. Smaller, less expensive vacuums may thus be adequate in some situations.

- *Vacuum hose:* Flow rates ranging from 50 to 80 CFM are best maintained with a 1½- to 2-inch diameter hose. If the diameter is larger, the airflow velocity of the vacuum will be reduced. If the diameter is smaller, airflow resistance will be higher. Airflow resistance also increases with hose length; excessively long hoses should be avoided. Many HEPA-filtered vacuum system kits include a variety of hose sizes for different tool applications.

- *Filters:* Double filtration is important. The use of a high-efficiency particulate air (HEPA) filter is critical to preventing the escape of respirable silica dust from the vacuum exhaust. HEPA filters are at least 99.97 percent efficient in removing fine particles of dust from the air. Vacuum cleaners with cyclonic pre-separators in addition to HEPA filters provide superior and cost-effective dust control when dust loading is high and high airflow is needed to capture and remove the dust. A cyclonic separator removes large particles that are capable of overloading or clogging the filter (Heitbrink and Collingwood, 2005).

- *Systematic cleaning:* Regular cleaning of the filter is critical to maintaining high airflow. Choose a vacuum equipped with a back-pulse filter cleaning cycle. Such auto-cleaning mechanisms will reduce the time required for vacuum maintenance and improve the overall efficiency of the dust collection system. If the vacuum does not have an auto-cleaning mechanism, the employee can periodically turn the vacuum cleaner on and off. This allows the bag to collapse and causes the prefilter cake to dislodge from the filter.

- *Monitoring VDC efficiency:* Purchasing a dust collection system equipped with a static pressure gauge allows the employee to monitor the system's efficiency. Systems lacking a static pressure gauge can be monitored visually. If a dust plume increases and becomes more visible where the exterior hood (suction ring) meets the working surface, the system is not working efficiently (Heitbrink and Collingwood, 2005).

System Maintenance. For optimal dust collection, the following measures are recommended:

- Keep the vacuum hose clear and free of debris, kinks and tight bends. Maintain the vacuum at peak performance to ensure adequate airflow through the dust collection device and vacuum hoses.

- Make sure that the vacuum bags and filters are changed regularly, as often as necessary to prevent a decrease in airflow. Dust escaping from the collection device can be a sign that airflow is inadequate.

- For best results, set up a regular schedule for filter cleaning and maintenance. For example, institute a rule to clean the filter or change the bag at each break. This will prevent pressure loss and ensure that exhaust airflow stays constant on the VDC system.

- Remember, the absence of visible dust does not necessarily mean that employees are adequately protected from silica exposure.

Dust Barriers

An employee who drills only an occasional small hole in the course of a day may have relatively low silica exposure. It is a good idea to minimize exposure to even small amounts of silica dust, so you might want to experiment with techniques for capturing dust from a single small hole initially developed in the asbestos abatement industry.

One simple dust control method involves inserting the drill bit through a barrier, which is then pressed against the working surface during drilling. The dust exiting the hole collects against the barrier. If the barrier is damp, it forms a better seal against the working surface and also moistens the dust, thus capturing more dust and reducing the amount that can escape when the employee removes the barrier. For example, employees sometimes drill through shaving cream in an upside-down waxed paper cup or through a damp sponge to minimize exposure to asbestos (U.S. GSA, 2001; Woods, 2000; LBL, undated).[4] These materials compress and are held in place by the pressure of the advancing drill. Assuming the barrier material can make a good connection with the surface, this method is appropriate for most materials that an employee might drill.

Tips for Devising a Dust Barrier for Occasional Drilling. For optimal results, the following measures are recommended:

- Insert the drill bit through the barrier until the tip is just visible, and then set the tip against the working surface in the correct position.

- Ensure that there are no gaps between the working surface and the barrier through which small particles can escape and become airborne.

- Withdraw the drill bit by pulling it through the barrier, so that the barrier collects any debris drawn out with the bit.

- Dispose of dust and debris after completing each hole. Handle the barrier carefully to minimize dust release.

- Add a moist material to the barrier to wet dust and minimize release during disposal.

- When using a cup, use waxed paper, which will compress under pressure, rather than Styrofoam, which will crack.

- Do not allow the barrier to become overloaded. For deeper holes, periodically check under the barrier; it may be necessary to clean or empty it before the hole is complete.

Compressed Air

The use of compressed air to clean surfaces or clothing is strongly discouraged. Using compressed air to clean work surfaces or clothing can significantly increase employee exposure, especially in enclosed and semi-enclosed spaces. Cleaning should be performed with a HEPA-filtered vacuum or by wet methods.

Wet Methods

Wet methods are generally not appropriate for use with electric rotary hammers unless the tools are designed for use in damp environments. Pneumatic drills, however, can be used for wet drilling, and some come equipped with a water feed capability.

While designed primarily for use in explosive atmospheres, water-fed pneumatic drills can also be used to control silica exposures (CS UNITEC, 2003).

Wet methods are usually the most effective way to control silica dust generated during construction activities because wet dust is less able to become or remain airborne. Although few specific data are available regarding wet methods for drilling small holes, studies have shown that drilling with water-fed bits or water spray at the bit-rock interface can substantially reduce respirable dust generated by rock drilling rigs (OSHA Case Files; Organiscak and Page, 1996; NIOSH, 1999).

OSHA believes that wet methods can also help control silica dust generated by smaller drills. Controlled tests with a large-impact breaker (jackhammer) showed that an efficiently-operated, retrofitted spray-type water-feed system reduced employee exposure to respirable silica (Zalk, 2000, 2002). Similarly, use of a water spray nozzle on a pneumatic chipper was found to reduce exposure to respirable silica dust by 70 percent (Sam, 2000). Given the lower energy of handheld drills, a properly implemented water-feed system should significantly lower silica concentrations.

To ensure that dust emissions are minimized, maintain the water supply equipment, including pumps, hoses and nozzles in good operating condition. Track the water usage rate for different types of jobs to predict the volume needed, and ensure that enough water is available during the task.[6]

Freezing Temperatures. Freezing temperatures complicate the use of water. Consider heating the local work area, if practical, to prevent ice from forming in the water-feed system. Large portable heating units are commonly used to heat commercial and sometimes road and highway projects. Drain the system when not in use. If water freezes on the ground, chip away the ice or use deicing compounds or sand to control the slipping hazard.

Electrical Safety. Use ground-fault circuit interrupters (GFCIs) and watertight, sealable electrical connectors for electric tools and equipment on construction sites (OSHA, 1996). These features are particularly important to employee safety in wet or damp areas, such as where water is used to control dust. Although an assured equipment grounding conductor program is an acceptable alternative to GFCIs, OSHA recommends that employers use GFCIs where possible because they afford better protection for employees. (See 29 CFR 1926.404(b)(1) for OSHA's ground-fault protection requirements.)

Fans

Fans are not effective dust control devices when used as the sole control method and should not be used as the primary method for managing dust. Fans can, however, be useful as a supplement to other control methods. Use fans in enclosed areas, such as bathrooms, where dust will build up due to poor air circulation.

For the best effect, set an exhaust fan (the bigger, the better) in an open window or external doorway so that the fan captures dust and blows it outside. Avoid positioning employees near the exhausted air. An exhaust fan works best if a second window or door across the room is opened to allow fresh air to enter.

Example: A four-foot square fan is placed in a window exhausting to outside the building at maximum fan speed. The fan will have the strongest capture capability directly in front of the fan face, but this quickly drops off. At two feet away from the fan, the capture capability is reduced to 50 percent and at four feet, the capture capability is reduced to seven percent of the capture capability at the fan face. If the distance between the work activity and fan face is greater than the length of the fan side (four feet), dust capture would probably not be effective (ACGIH, 2007).

Case Studies

The following case studies indicate silica exposure levels found under certain uncontrolled conditions, and show the effectiveness of controls in reducing silica exposures.

Case Study I: Three construction workers used pneumatic and electric drills with ¾-inch bits to drill holes in the lower level of a concrete parking structure with poor ventilation. The employees used no dust control methods and their silica exposure levels ranged from 0.1 mg/m³ to 0.3 mg/m³ (Lofgren, 1993).[7]

Case Study II: In an older Swedish study, an employee used 6-millimeter (mm) bits to drill numerous holes 50-mm deep (approximately ¼-inch by 2-inch holes) into concrete under experimental conditions. Without dust controls, the average respirable silica exposure level was greater than 0.24 mg/m³ during the period evaluated. When a dust extraction system was added to the drill, the average respirable silica exposure was reduced to less than 0.095 mg/m³.[8] Investigators obtained similar results when they tested equipment with 10-mm bits used for drilling 80-mm deep holes (approxi-

mately ⅜ inch by 3⅛ inch). In this case, average exposure decreased from 0.3 mg/m³ (no controls) to less than 0.06 mg/m³ when dust extraction equipment was used (Hallin, 1983).[9]

In the same study, the operator tested equipment with a dust collection bag attached directly to the drill. This condition had some of the highest exposures reported for drilling with dust controls.[10] The exposures were substantially lower than the levels reported for uncontrolled drilling, but two of the three results exceeded 0.1 mg/m³ (Hallin, 1983).

Respiratory Protection and Engineering Control Evaluation

Using a rotary hammer or similar tool without engineering controls can cause exposures to respirable crystalline silica to reach 0.3 mg/m³ or higher as an 8-hour time-weighted average. During periods of active drilling, exposures can reach as high as 0.78 mg/m³ without controls. Therefore, it is important to utilize effective controls to reduce employee exposures.

Both VDC systems and wet methods are generally effective in controlling exposures to below 0.1 mg/m³. However, wet methods are not appropriate with electric rotary hammers that are not designed to be used in wet environments. In these cases, VDC systems offer the better option of control.

If the rotary hammer is being controlled by a VDC system or wet methods, then respiratory protection may not be necessary. However, where employee exposure exceeds 0.1 mg/m³ it may be necessary to use a properly fitted, NIOSH-approved half-facepiece or disposable respirator equipped with an N-, R- or P-95 filter to supplement use of the VDC system or wet methods methods (see 29 CFR 1926.103).

In any workplace where respirators are necessary to protect the health of the employee, or whenever respirators are required by the employer, the employer must establish and implement a written respiratory protection program with worksite-specific procedures and elements, including the selection of respirators, medical evaluations of employees, fit testing, proper usage, maintenance and care, cleaning and disinfecting, proper air quality/quantity and training (see 29 CFR 1926.103).

Construction sites often involve many operations occurring simultaneously that can generate respirable silica dust. Therefore, it is important and necessary to utilize effective controls (such as wet methods or VDC) in order to minimize total exposures to silica-exposed tool operators.

Employers should conduct exposure monitoring periodically while controls are being used to ensure that the controls are working properly and that the appropriate level of respiratory protection is being used.

For more information on how to determine proper respiratory protection, visit OSHA's Web site at www.osha.gov. NIOSH's Web site also provides information on respirators at www.cdc.gov/niosh.

References

ACGIH. 2007. Industrial Ventilation, a Manual of Recommended Practice, 26th edition. American Conference of Governmental Industrial Hygienists, Cincinnati, OH, 2001.

ACGIH. 2008. Threshold limit values for chemical substances and physical agents and biological exposure indices. American Conference of Governmental Industrial Hygienists, Cincinnati. OH, 2008.

CS UNITEC. 2003. Air Rotary Hammer Drill. http://www.csunitec.com/ rotary/airrotary.html. Accessed January 13, 2003.

Hallin, N. 1983. Occurrence of quartz in the construction sector (Report 1983-04-01). Bygghälsan—The construction industry's organization for working environment, safety and health. Stockholm, Sweden. April 1, 1983.

Heitbrink, W.A. and D.S. Watkins. 2001. The effect of exhaust flow rate upon the respirable dust emissions for tuckpointing operations. In: In-Depth Study Report: Control Technology for Crystalline Silica Exposures in Construction. U.S. Department of Health and Human Services, Centers for Disease Control and Prevention, National Institute for Occupational Safety and Health. ECTB No. 247-18, 2001.

Heitbrink, W. and Collingwood, S. 2005. Protecting Tuckpointing Workers from Silica Dust: Draft Recommendations for Ventilated Grinder. The Center to Protect Workers' Rights (CPWR). www.cpwr.com

LBL. Undated. Asbestos management program, appendix G, Bulk sampling procedure. Lawrence Berkeley National Laboratory. Berkeley, CA.: http://www.lbl.gov/ehs/ih/forms/AsbesProg.doc. Accessed January 13, 2003.

Lofgren, D.J. 1993. Silica exposure for concrete workers and masons. Appl. Occup. Environ. Hyg. 8(10):832-836, 1993.

NIOSH. 1996. Preventing silicosis and deaths in construction workers. U.S. Dept. of Health and Human Services (National Institute for Occupational Safety and Health, Publication No. 96-112). Cincinnati, OH.

NIOSH. 1999. Control technology and exposure assessment for occupational exposure to crystalline silica: Case 22 – rock drilling (ECTB 233-122c). National Institute for Occupational Safety and Health, Cincinnati, OH. November 19, 1999.

NIOSH. 2002. Pocket guide to chemical hazards. Pub. No. 2002-140. National Institute for Occupational Safety and Health, Cincinnati, OH. June.

Organiscak, J.A. and S.J. Page. 1996. Assessment of airborne dust generated from small truck-mounted rock drills. Report of Investigation No. 9616. U.S. Department of the Interior, Bureau of Mines, Pittsburgh, PA.

OSHA Case Files (Special Emphasis Program Inspection Reports from 1996-1998).

Sam, K. 2000. Control measures for reducing employee exposure to concentrations of total and respirable silica in the ready-mix concrete industry during drum cleaning. Presentation at American Industrial Hygiene Conference & Exposition. Orlando, FL. May 24, 2000.

Shepherd, S., Woskie, S.R., Holcroft, C. and Ellenbecker, M. 2009. Reducing Silica and Dust Exposures in Construction During Use of Powered Concrete-Cutting Hand Tools: Efficacy of Local Exhaust Ventilation on Hammer Drills. Journal of Occupational and Environmental Hygiene, 6:1,42-51, 2009.

U.S. GSA. 2001. Standard operating procedure for asbestos operations and maintenance activities. Appendix B: Cleaning above a drop ceiling--mini-containment methods. U.S. General Services Administration, Kansas City, MO. July. http://safety.gsa.gov/gsa/heartland/sops/acm_sop.pdf. Accessed January 13, 2003.

Woods, David T. 2000. A common sense approach to disturbing asbestos. Ind. Safety & Hyg. News Online. www.ishn.com/CDA/ArticleInformation/features/BNP___Features___Item/0,2162,2572,00.html. Accessed January 15, 2003.

Zalk, D. 2000. Presentation at American Industrial Hygiene Conference & Exposition. Orlando, FL. May 24, 2000.

Zalk, D. 2002. Personal communication between D. Zalk, Lawrence Livermore Laboratory, CA, and W. Long, Eastern Research Group, Inc., Arlington, VA. October 29, 2002.

Technical Notes

[1] The three respirable crystalline silica results cited are 0.3, 0.26, and 0.11 mg/m³, collected as 457-, 110- and 177-minute samples, respectively (Lofgren, 1993).

[2] Laboratories have not used particle counting for crystalline silica analysis in many years and now report exposure data gravimetrically. However, OSHA's construction PEL for crystalline silica, established in 1971, is still listed as a particle-count value. (See Appendix E to OSHA's National Emphasis Program for Crystalline Silica, CPL 03-00-007, for a detailed discussion of the conversion factor used to transform gravimetric measurements to particle-count values). In this guidance, OSHA is using 0.1 mg/m³ of respirable quartz as an 8-hour time-weighted average as a benchmark to describe the effectiveness of control measures. The benchmark is approximately equivalent to the general industry silica PEL. Other organizations suggest more stringent levels. For example, the National Institute for Occupational Safety and Health (NIOSH) recommends that respirable crystalline silica exposures be limited to 0.05 mg/m³ as a 10-hour time-weighted average (NIOSH, 2002). The American Conference of Governmental Industrial Hygienists (ACGIH) recommends that respirable crystalline silica exposures be limited to 0.025 mg/m³ as an 8-hour time-weighted average (ACGIH, 2008).

[3] This short-term respirable crystalline silica sample was collected over a 45-minute period (NIOSH, 1996).

[4] This technique, widely used for drilling asbestos-containing materials, would also help control respirable silica-containing dust.

[5] Water-fed drilling can include using small amounts of water introduced into bailing air to suppress dust and cool the bit, or water used instead of air to flush debris from the hole. These studies indicate that combining wet methods with local exhaust ventilation achieves even greater exposure reduction than wet-methods alone.

[6] Bit size, hole depth, substrate and weather all affect the amount of water needed to control dust. The usage rate must be adjusted for each individual operation. For drill rigs with water injected into bailing air, about ½ to 1 gallon per minute is sufficient (Organiscak and Page, 1996).

[7] A bulk dust sample showed silica content of 12 percent in the concrete being drilled. During the 110- to 457-minute periods monitored, the employees' silica exposures ranged from 0.11 mg/m³ to 0.3 mg/m³, with a median of 0.26 mg/m³.

[8] Uncontrolled case for 6-mm bit: n = 6, median = 0.14 mg/m³, and range = 0.06 - 0.81 mg/m³. Controlled case: n = 9, median = 0.08 mg/m³, and range = 0.03 - 0.29 mg/m³. Reported results are for the 90- to 120-minute periods monitored. The lower exposure levels may be due, in part, to the fact that the employee in the controlled case drilled fewer holes with each test drill while using dust collection equipment, approximately 30 to 40 holes. Without controls the employee drilled 40 to 90 holes with each drill (Hallin, 1983).

[9] Uncontrolled case with 10-mm drill bit: n = 4, median = 0.295 mg/m³, and range = 0.28 - 0.33 mg/m³: Controlled case with 10 mm bit: n = 10, median = 0.045 mg/m³, and range = 0.04 - 0.14 mg/m³. All sample durations were either 120 or 180 minutes (Hallin, 1983).

[10] Of the three results for 120-minute samples associated with dust collection bags attached directly to drills (0.04, 0.11 and 0.13 mg/m³), two exceeded 0.1 mg/m³ and were among the highest 15 percent of the 40 results obtained during controlled drilling (Hallin, 1983).

Vehicle-Mounted Rock Drilling Rigs

This section covers drills mounted on trucks, crawlers and other vehicles when used for drilling rock or soil. The term "silica" used in this document refers to respirable crystalline silica.

Introduction

Exposure to fine particles of silica has been shown to cause silicosis, a serious and sometimes fatal lung disease. Construction employees who inhale fine particles of silica may be at risk of developing this disease. Employees produce dusts containing silica when they use rock-drilling rigs mounted on trucks, crawlers or other vehicles to drill into rock, concrete, or soil. The small particles easily become suspended in the air and, when inhaled, penetrate deep into employees' lungs.

Studies have shown that drilling into rock, concrete, or soil may produce hazardous levels of respirable silica if measures are not taken to limit and control dust emissions. The National Institute for Occupational Safety and Health (NIOSH), for example, found that a drilling rig operator at a construction site was exposed to 0.54 mg/m^3 (milligrams of silica per cubic meter of air) over the course of a day (NIOSH, 1992b).

This level is more than five times the Occupational Safety and Health Administration's (OSHA) benchmark of 0.1 mg/m^3 (milligrams per cubic meter of air) as an 8-hour time-weighted average (TWA), an exposure approximately equivalent to OSHA's general industry permissible exposure limit (PEL).[1] Furthermore, the U.S. Bureau of Mines found that respirable silica concentrations averaged 2.13 mg/m^3 in the immediate vicinity of small surface drilling operations (U.S. Bureau of Mines, 1995).

Concentrations of respirable silica in soil and rock may vary widely depending on the type of underlying rock formation and history of volcanic eruptions. For example, the preliminary site investigation of the Department of Energy's Yucca Mountain site indicated that soil concentrations of cristobalite (a form of silica) ranged from 18 to 28 percent, and many job tasks were associated with overexposure (CRWMS 1999). If a construction company will be doing substantial excavation at a site, then obtaining a profile of the silica content of soil and rock from bulk samples of the projected excavation represents good industrial hygiene practice. Many times this information can be obtained as part of the project design and provided to the contractor as part of the description of existing site conditions.

This section describes methods available to reduce employees' exposures to silica when using vehicle-mounted drilling rigs. The three primary methods used to reduce dust emissions during rock drilling are dust collection systems, wet methods and operator isolation. OSHA recommends that these drills always be operated using a combination of dust control techniques.

Earth drilling rigs operated without dust controls are capable of producing very high respirable silica levels (Photo courtesy of NIOSH, 1992.)

Silica Dust Control Measures

Dust Collection Systems

Various types of dust collection systems are available for earth drills. Commonly used equipment incorporates a movable suction duct attached to a shroud (a flexible rubber skirt) that encloses the drill hole opening and captures the cuttings coming through the hole. Drilling equipment that does not include these controls can be retrofitted by the manufacturer or a mechanical shop.

Dusty air pulled from the shroud enclosure usually passes through a flexible duct leading to a primary dust separator and a secondary filter system. The dust separator often includes a self-cleaning "back-pulse" feature that discharges the collected particles to the ground. Some secondary filter systems are also self-cleaning. Finally, the exhaust air is discharged to the atmosphere.

Design Considerations

Dust collection systems are commercially available and work well in all climates and with all drill types. If the systems are well designed, dust collectors offer substantial dust reduction. Some important design factors are described below.

Drill Bit Shroud Design. Conventional shrouds are rectangular and constructed of four separate pieces of rubber attached to the drill platform. Dust can escape from each open seam or gap. Designs that minimize the number of flaps and gaps can help improve dust capture.

NIOSH tested a circular, slightly conical shroud design that reduced gaps through which dust could escape. Steel banding attached the shroud to the drill deck, closed the single seam and helped hold the shroud's shape. A small trap door in the test shroud allowed employees to shovel cuttings from inside without distorting or lifting the shroud, actions which can reduce dust collection efficiency. Keeping cuttings cleared away is always important for maintaining good contact between the bottom of a shroud and the ground. In the tests, the single-seam conical shroud captured dust more efficiently (99 percent) than a conventional square-shaped shroud (95 percent) (NIOSH, 1998).

Adequate Airflow. The dust collector must be designed to draw more air volume than the bailing air volume used to flush cuttings from the drill hole. To capture all the bailing air and dust using a conventional shroud, the airflow rate for the dust collector should be a minimum of three times the bailing airflow rate (NIOSH, 1998). Improved shroud designs may require somewhat less air, while less efficient shrouds may require more. Air volume is generally measured in cubic feet per minute (CFM).

Dust Collector Discharge Shrouds. A shroud or sleeve enclosing the dust collection hopper discharge door can help reduce dust emissions. During the dumping cycle, the sleeve guides particles to the ground, thereby reducing dust that would otherwise become airborne as material falls to the ground. Heavy tarps or extendable coil-type flexible duct materials make effective shrouds.

Tests of discharge door shrouds showed an 81 percent reduction in airborne dust during the dump cycle (Page and Organiscak, 1995). Remember to control material dumped from filter cartridges as well. If possible, discharge this dust at a distance from employees (OSHA Case File).

Exhaust Air Discharge Design. Dust exposures can be further reduced by extending the primary dust collection system exhaust port to release the air farther away from employees. After an eight-foot vertical PVC pipe was installed on the discharge port, a test showed that airborne respirable dust concentrations 100 feet downwind of the drill were reduced by 62 percent (Organiscak and Page, 1996). Extending the exhaust pipe away from employees becomes particularly important if a secondary filter is not used to capture the respirable silica particles.

If a flexible duct is extended near ground level, avoid placing the opening where the exhausted air will blow on other employees (including those downwind). Instead, place the duct opening near the ground where exhausted dust might deposit. To minimize airflow resistance in the flexible duct, run extensions in a relatively straight line, use the same diameter as the discharge flexible duct and keep added lengths to the minimum needed to move the discharged air away from employees.

Maintenance Considerations

Dust collectors require routine care to ensure that they are functioning as designed. Equipment that is not well maintained can contribute to employee exposure. Check the following points on a regular basis.

Close Gaps in Shroud. To be effective, a shroud must fully enclose the bit. Make sure that the shroud on your equipment is in good condition. Repair or replace torn or missing pieces and ensure that gaps seal well. Tests show that simply maintaining the shroud in good condition can reduce dust exposures by over 60 percent (Organiscak and Page, 1996). For best results, lift the shroud as little as possible.

If a well-maintained, well-sealed shroud leaks dust, the airflow might be inadequate. Check the condition of filters, the blower and ducts which are possible causes of inadequate airflow.

Duct and Filter Maintenance. Clogged flexible ducts and filters restrict dust collector airflow. Visually inspect flexible ducts and filters often and stay alert to signs of reduced flow (for example, an increase in dust escaping from the shroud). Remove material that accumulates in the flexible ducts; deposited dust both restricts airflow and could be a sign of filter or blower problems.[2]

If filters have an automatic cleaning cycle, be sure that it is functioning as intended. Replace clogged or damaged filters. During one drilling rig evaluation, dust collector air suction was increased from 2,165 CFM to 3,370 CFM when new filters were installed (Page, 1991).

Fan Maintenance. Abrasive dust is destructive to the fan motor, blades and drill bits. Routine maintenance is important for both. Experts recommend scheduled inspections to check the following points on the fan blower unit (ACGIH, 2001):

- Bearings and lubrication;
- Belt tension, wear and slippage;
- Excessive vibration;
- Coupling and belt alignment;

- Fan impeller alignment and rotation;
- Excessive wear or caking on the impeller;
- Mounting bolts, set screws and bushings; and
- Safety guards.

Visible and Respirable Dust

Visible dust contains large particles that are easy to see. The tiny, respirable-sized particles (those that can get into the deep lung) containing silica pose the greatest hazard and are not visible. Most dust-generating construction activities produce a mixture of visible and respirable particles.

Do use visible dust as a general guide for improving dust suppression efforts. If you see visible dust being generated, emissions of respirable silica are probably too high. Measures that control tool-generated dust at the source usually reduce *all* types of particle emissions, including respirable particles.

Do not rely *only* on visible dust to assess the extent of the silica hazard. There may be airborne respirable dust present that is not visible to the naked eye.

Wet Methods

The proper use of wet methods requires a skilled operator. In wet drilling, too much water can create mud slurry at the bottom of the hole that can entrap the bit, coupling and steel extensions. Too little water will not effectively control dust emissions. Studies indicate that the optimal water flow rate is best achieved by slowly increasing the water to the point where visible dust emissions are eliminated (Organiscak and Page, 1996).[3]

While water injection methods work well for percussion, drag and button bits, special consideration is required to protect bits with rollers (tri-cone bits) from excess water on moving parts. A water separator described by the U.S. Bureau of Mines removed all water except a slight mist from the bailing air, which improves dust control as explained below (Page, 1991).

Water Injection at Bit. In wet drilling systems that use forced air to flush cuttings from the hole, water is introduced into the bailing air at the drill head. The water serves to gather the small particles into larger ones, thus reducing dust emissions. One study of dust emissions during drilling found that wet drilling was 29 percent more effective in reducing airborne respirable dust in the immediate drill vicinity (where the operator would typically stand) than a conventional dust collection system without water (Organiscak and Page, 1996).

Wet drilling combined with a conventional dust collection system offers even better dust control. One exposure survey of rock drilling operations showed that the combination of wet drilling with a dust collection system resulted in a 42 percent reduction in an operator's respirable dust exposure when compared to wet drilling alone (Zimmer, 1997).[4]

Water Injection at Dust Collector Exhaust. Tests have shown that injecting small quantities of water into the exhaust air discharge duct significantly reduces respirable silica dust emissions. In a drill site experiment, investigators placed a water tank at a location suitable for a gravity feed and coupled it to the exhaust air discharge port using ¼-inch flexible tubing and a needle valve. Then they turned the exhaust port so that it was slanting down and added a 20-foot flexible duct that was also slightly downward sloping, ending about one foot above the ground, to allow material to fall out the end. Water was trickled into the flexible duct at a rate of one gallon per five minutes (0.2 gallons/minute) (Organiscak and Page, 1996).[5,6]

When adding water to the discharge flexible duct of the dust collection system, it is important not to use too much, to avoid clogging problems. The flow rate should be slowly increased until visible dust emissions are significantly reduced. For better control, it is recommended that two valves be used to adjust the water flow, one as a flow regulator and the second as the on/off control. Add an in-line water filter to keep debris in the water from blocking the needle valve (NIOSH, 1997).

Even at ideal water flow rates, it will be necessary to check the flexible duct interior daily and clear dust deposits that may form in it. A quick-release clamp on the flexible duct will make the process easier (Organiscak, 2002).

Operator Isolation

Drill operators using rigs with enclosed cabs can reduce their potential silica exposure by spending as much time as possible inside the vehicle cab while drilling is in progress. To be effective, the cab must be well sealed and ventilated. Door jams, window grooves, power line entries and other joints should be tightly sealed. Provide a slight positive pressure, using filtered air, to prevent dust from leaking into the cab. For the best dust control, use a high-efficiency particulate air (HEPA) filter. Some equipment permits the operation of the drill from inside the cab.

An exposure survey found that if operators spend time inside a fully enclosed cab and use wet drilling together with a dust collection system, dust exposures can be reduced up to 76 percent when compared to wet drilling alone (Zimmer, 1997).

While the use of enclosed cabs substantially reduces silica exposures, operators might be unwilling to keep windows and doors closed if the cab is not air conditioned. Equipment might be upgraded by installing aftermarket ventilation and air conditioning systems.[7]

Even in a sealed cab, dust already inside the cab can become airborne. Clean cabs daily to remove dust tracked in on boots or settled on surfaces.

Combining Methods for Better Dust Control

To effectively protect employees, dust control is necessary at multiple points in the drilling process. Table 1, below, summarizes the common sources of airborne dust and the dust management methods described in this section. Most of these techniques can be used together to enhance employee protection from silica exposures.

Table 1: Summary of Dust Control Techniques for Vehicle-Mounted Rock Drilling	
Source of Dust	**Control Techniques**
Primary Source: Dust released from drill hole	• Use wetdrilling/water injection methods • Install dust collector
Dust escaping from dust collector shroud	• Maintain shroud condition • Close gaps in shroud • Avoid lifting or distorting the shroud during drilling • Clear away cuttings • Increase airflow rate
Airborne dust released from dust separator and filter cartridge discharge port	• Add a shroud to discharge door • Inject water into dust collector discharge • Install a filter bag over cartridge filter dump discharge point
Fine particles in exhaust air from dust collector	• Extend flexible duct to release air at a distance from employees
Uncontrolled dust from drilling and other nearby activities	• Use enclosed cab with filtered air • Stay upwind of dust sources, when possible • Watch for sources of dust and make adjustments as needed

Table 2, below, ranks the efficacy of various combinations of available control technology for rock drilling rigs and reflects the judgment of OSHA's contract consultant, ERG, based on their literature review (ERG, 2003).

Table 2: Rating Dust Control Methods for Vehicle-Mounted Rock Drilling Rigs	
Control Method	**Rating**
Wet drilling + dust collection system + operator's cab	*****
Wet drilling + dust collecting system	****
Wet drilling + operator's cab	****
Wet drilling	***
Dust collection system	***
No control	*

*= poor   *****= excellent

Ratings are based on the method's ability to efficiently capture respirable dust and reliably control employees' exposure.

Source: ERG, 2003.

Work Practices

Proper work practices are also important in reducing potential silica exposures.

*   When possible, equipment should be positioned so that operators and others can work upwind from a drill's dust emissions.

*   Put dust control equipment on a regular maintenance schedule.

*   Train employees to watch for sources of dust and to make necessary adjustments or repairs to reduce emissions – and their own exposure.

Case Studies

The following case studies indicate silica exposure levels found under certain uncontrolled conditions, and show the effectiveness of controls in reducing silica exposures.

No Dust Controls. NIOSH evaluated silica exposure for an employee dry-drilling rock when the drill's dust collector was out of operation. The 5½-hour sample indicated that the drill operator's exposure was 0.54 mg/m³ when averaged over an 8-hour shift. If the operator had continued the same work for the full 8 hours, his respirable silica exposure would have been 0.80 mg/m³, which greatly exceeds allowable levels (NIOSH, 1992b).

Multiple Dust Controls. In contrast, at another construction site employees used multiple drills with various dust controls to prepare granite for blasting.[8] OSHA measured a full-shift exposure level of 0.054 mg/m^3 (half the PEL) for an operator using a water-injected drill fitted with a two-stage dust collector.

This construction company used combined dust controls to keep exposures consistently below the PEL for all drill operators and their assistants (OSHA Case File).[9]

Compressed Air

The use of compressed air to clean surfaces or clothing is strongly discouraged. Using compressed air to clean work surfaces or clothing can significantly increase employee exposure, especially in enclosed and semi-enclosed spaces. Cleaning should be performed with a HEPA-filtered vacuum or by wet methods.

Respiratory Protection and Engineering Control Evaluation

Operating a rock drilling rig without engineering controls can cause exposures to respirable silica to reach 0.8 mg/m^3 or higher (NIOSH, 1992b). Effective controls, such as dust collection systems, wet methods and operator isolation can reduce exposures.

Operators of rock drilling rigs working in enclosed, well-ventilated and sealed cabs should not experience silica exposures in excess of 0.1 mg/m^3 as an 8-hour time-weighted average. However, those operators and helpers working outside of cabs, or those using cabs which are not enclosed, well-ventilated and sealed, can experience elevated exposures. OSHA estimates that exposures would not normally exceed 1.0 mg/m^3 with appropriate wet methods or dust collection systems in place. Therefore, in addition to the controls, the operators and helpers working in these conditions may need to wear a properly fitted, NIOSH-approved half-facepiece or disposable respirator with an N-, R- or P-95 filter. Such protection is adequate for exposures up to 1.0 mg/m^3. Where exposures exceed 1.0 mg/m^3, higher levels of respiratory protection are necessary (see 29 CFR 1926.103).

Since exposures may not be controlled to below 0.1 mg/m^3 even with wet methods and/or dust collection systems, employees in close proximity to the work operation where silica dust is generated may need respiratory protection. The level of respiratory protection is dependent on the employee's silica exposure, which varies depending on factors in the work environment (such as enclosed, semi-enclosed, or open spaces and/or multiple operations generating silica dust), environmental conditions (such as wind direction and speed) and the percentage of silica found in the material.

In any workplace where respirators are necessary to protect the health of the employee, or whenever respirators are required by the employer, the employer must establish and implement a written respiratory protection program with worksite-specific procedures and elements. These should include the selection of respirators, medical evaluations of employees, fit testing, proper usage, maintenance and care, cleaning and disinfecting, proper air quality/quantity and training (see 29 CFR 1926.103).

Employers should conduct exposure monitoring periodically while controls are being used to ensure that the controls are working properly and that the appropriate level of respiratory protection is being used.

For more information on how to determine proper respiratory protection, visit OSHA's Web site at www.osha.gov. NIOSH's Web site also provides information on respirators at www.cdc.gov/niosh.

References

ACGIH. 2001. Industrial Ventilation, A Manual of Recommended Practice. 24th Edition. American Conference of Governmental Industrial Hygienists. Cincinnati, OH, 2001.

ACGIH. 2008. Threshold limit values for chemical substances and physical agents and biological exposure indices. American Conference of Governmental Industrial Hygienists, Cincinnati, OH, 2008.

CRWMS. 1999. Engineering File – Subsurface Repository. Civilian Radioactive Waste Management System Management & Operating Contractor. BCA000000-01717-5705-00005 Rev 02, DCN 01. June, 1999.

ERG. 2003. Technological Feasibility Study and Cost Impact Analysis of the Draft Crystalline Silica Standard for Construction. Table 2, Ranking of dust control technology, ERG composite of available research on control technology. February, 2003.

NIOSH ALERT, 1992a. Preventing Silicosis and Deaths in Rock Drillers. No. 92-107.

NIOSH. 1992b. Environmental surveillance report: Breckinridge Construction Drilling, Westover, WV. National Institute for Occupational Safety and Health, Division of Respiratory Disease Studies, Morgantown, WV, 1992.

NIOSH. 1997. Silica...it's not just dust – What rock-drillers can do to protect their lungs from silica dust. U.S. Dept. of Health and Human Services (National Institute for Occupational Safety and Health, Publication No. 97-118), available at <http://www. cdc. gov/niosh/rock.html>. Accessed November 22, 2002.

NIOSH. 1998. New shroud design controls silica dust for surface mine and construction blast-hole drills. U.S. Dept. of Health and Human Services (National Institute for Occupational Safety and Health, Publication No. 98-150), 1998.

NIOSH. 2002. Pocket guide to chemical hazards. Pub. No. 2002-140. National Institute for Occupational Safety and Health, Cincinnati, OH. June, 2002.

Organiscak, J.A. 2002. Personal communication between J. Organiscak, National Institute for Occupational Safety and Health, Pittsburgh, PA, and W. Long of Eastern Research Group, Inc. November 21, 2002.

Organiscak, J.A. and S.J. Page. 1996. Assessment of airborne dust generated from small truck-mounted rock drills. Report of investigation No. 9616. U.S. Department of the Interior, Bureau of Mines, Pittsburgh, PA, 1996.

OSHA Case Files (Special Emphasis Program Inspection Reports from 1996-1998).

Page, S.J. 1991. Respirable dust control on overburdened drills at surface mines. American Mining Congress, Coal Convention. June 5, 1991.

Page, S.J. and J.A. Organiscak. 1995. Taming the dust devil: an evaluation of improved dust controls for surface drills using Rotoclone collectors. Engineering and Mining Journal, pp. ww30 – ww31. November, 1995.

U.S. Bureau of Mines. 1995. Dust collector discharge shroud reduces dust exposure to drill operators at surface coal mines. Technology News. No. 447. March, 1995.

Zimmmer, A.T. 1997. Comparative evolution of dust control technologies on percussion rock-drilling rigs. Appl. Occup. Environ. Hyg. 12(12): 782-788. December, 1997.

Technical Notes

[1] Laboratories have not used particle counting for crystalline silica analysis in many years and now report exposure data gravimetrically. However, OSHA's construction PEL for crystalline silica, established in 1971, is still listed as a particle-count value.

(See Appendix E to OSHA's National Emphasis Program for Crystalline Silica, CPL 03-00-007, for a detailed discussion of the conversion factor used to transform gravimetric measurements to particle-count values). In this guidance, OSHA is using 0.1 mg/m^3 of respirable quartz as an 8-hour time-weighted average as a benchmark to describe the effectiveness of control measures. The benchmark is approximately equivalent to the general industry silica PEL. Other organizations suggest more stringent levels. For example, the National Institute for Occupational Safety and Health (NIOSH) recommends that respirable crystalline silica exposures be limited to 0.05 mg/m^3 as a 10-hour time-weighted average (NIOSH, 2002). The American Conference of Governmental Industrial Hygienists (ACGIH) recommends that respirable crystalline silica exposures be limited to 0.025 mg/m^3 as an 8-hour time-weighted average (ACGIH, 2008).

[2] To avoid clogging, ACGIH (2001) recommends 3,500 to 4,000 feet per minute (FPM) minimum air velocity through ducts carrying rock or concrete dust. Use a higher velocity of at least 4,500 FPM if dust is moist or contains small chips.

[3] Bit size, hole depth, substrate and weather all affect the amount of water needed to control dust. The usage rate must be adjusted for each individual operation, but typically will be about ½ to 1 gallon per minute.

[4] Certain drill systems use large quantities of water, rather than air, to flush cuttings from the hole. The large volume of water in the hole usually controls dust completely and additional devices, such as dust collectors, offer very little extra benefit.

[5] High air velocity and turbulence in the flexible duct atomize the water drops to create a mist, which captures dust as it moves down the length of the duct (Organiscak, 2002).

[6] To measure water flow rate, adjust the flow as desired, then check how long it takes to fill a one-gallon milk container.

[7] To better exclude dust, pressurize the cab interior by using a pressurization unit to introduce filtered outside air into the cab. Studies show that 100 cubic feet per minute (CFM) provides adequate pressure (0.2 inches of water gauge) to keep dust from leaking into a well-sealed 100 cubic foot cab.

[8] Bulk samples indicated the granite contained 30 to 40 percent crystalline silica.

[9] Seven full-shift samples collected over six months. Air-sampling data collected by OSHA and a company consultant were consistently below 0.061 mg/m^3, with an average exposure level of 0.032 mg/m^3 (OSHA Case File).

Drywall Finishing

This section describes methods of controlling silica exposures during drywall finishing tasks. The term "silica" used in this document refers to respirable crystalline silica.

Introduction

Exposure to fine particles of silica has been shown to cause silicosis, a serious and sometimes fatal lung disease. Construction employees who inhale fine particles of silica may be at risk of developing this disease. Even when dust does not contain silica, employees performing dusty jobs may be at risk. Excessive exposure to airborne dust can contribute to tissue injury in the eyes, ears and respiratory passages.

When sanding drywall joint compound, employees generate a substantial amount of airborne dust. The smallest dust particles – the respirable particles – are hazardous because they are deposited deep in the lungs (Murray, J. and Nadel, J., 1994). Dust that contains silica presents a particularly dangerous hazard, but exposure to high levels of dust, whether or not it contains silica, can also be harmful to health. To avoid potentially hazardous exposures, employers should implement effective dust control measures during all drywall finishing activities.

The primary method for avoiding silica exposure, and thereby eliminating the risk of developing silicosis, is to use only silica-free joint compounds. Drywall finishers can also reduce their dust exposure by using vacuum dust collection equipment or wet sanding methods.

Visible and Respirable Dust

Visible dust contains large particles that are easy to see. The tiny, respirable-sized particles (those that can get into the deep lung) containing silica pose the greatest hazard and are not visible. Most dust-generating construction activities produce a mixture of visible and respirable particles.

Do use visible dust as a general guide for improving dust suppression efforts. If you see visible dust being generated, emissions of respirable silica are probably too high. Measures that control tool-generated dust at the source usually reduce *all* types of particle emissions, including respirable particles.

Do not rely *only* on visible dust to assess the extent of the silica hazard. There may be airborne respirable dust present that is not visible to the naked eye.

Drywall Finishing Employees' Exposures

The silica exposures of drywall finishing employees are typically well below allowable limits, primarily due to the low silica content of joint compounds. Nonetheless, drywall joint compounds may contain varying amounts of silica and drywall finishing employees can be overexposed in certain circumstances. For example, by using a joint compound containing just 3 percent silica, an employee could exceed the Occupational Safety and Health Administration's (OSHA) benchmark of 0.1 mg/m³ (milligrams of silica per cubic meter of air) as an 8-hour time-weighted average (TWA), an exposure approximately equivalent to OSHA's general industry permissible exposure limit (PEL), during intensive periods of uncontrolled drywall sanding on ceilings. One study of drywall sanding, in which a silica-containing joint compound was used, found that the respirable silica level exceeded 0.15 mg/m³ (NIOSH, 1997).[1,2]

The potential for silica exposure is also indicated by the results of NIOSH tests of settled drywall dust. NIOSH found that dust generated during drywall sanding contained up to 6 percent silica (NIOSH, 1995). Other studies found that silica constituted up to 3.7 percent of the airborne respirable dust collected in drywall sanding employees' breathing zones (NIOSH, 1997; Epling et al., 1999).[3]

Drywall sanding employees can also experience total dust exposures substantially above OSHA limits. In one study, employees using hand sanders without controls had exposures up to 143.1 mg/m³ of total dust. Similarly, employees using conventional pole-mounted sanders were exposed to up to 35.1 mg/m³ of total dust (CPWR, 1998).[4]

Although both of these exposures exceed regulatory limits, these results demonstrate that pole sander use can reduce dust exposures by increasing the distance between the employee and the point of work. An earlier NIOSH study also found lower exposures for employees using pole-mounted drywall sanders compared to handheld sanding (NIOSH, 1995).

Additionally, NIOSH (1997) found that some of the highest dust exposures occur when employees sand joint compound in enclosed spaces, such as closets or small rooms. Poor air exchange in these areas causes dust levels to build up when dust controls are not used.

Increasing or decreasing dust dissipation (by increasing distance to the employee or decreasing air exchange) affects respirable dust levels as well as total dust levels. For example, concrete finishers using a long-angled jig to grind a ceiling had lower silica exposures than employees grinding concrete with equipment attached to a short section of pipe and held directly overhead (OSHA Case Files). Employees grinding concrete indoors had higher respirable silica exposures than employees performing the same task outdoors, where dust could dissipate more quickly (Lofgren, 1993; NIOSH, 2001; OSHA Case Files).

Silica-Free Joint Compounds

Many manufacturers offer joint compounds that contain little or no silica. In a study of six brands of joint compound purchased at retail stores, no crystalline silica was detected in three brands (NIOSH, 1997). The silica present in a sample of one of the six products, however, was substantially different from the percentage listed on the material safety data sheet (MSDS) for that product.[5] Nonetheless, OSHA recommends that employers rely on manufacturers' information and use proper methods to minimize employees' dust exposures, rather than testing joint compounds themselves.

Regardless of a compound's silica content, the high levels of dust that drywall finishing may generate also poses a health hazard. Thus, OSHA recommends that employees always use dust control measures when drywall sanding. The two principal methods for controlling dust are (1) vacuum dust collection systems and (2) wet sponging. Either method is easy to implement.

Silica-Free Joint Compounds
- Check the label and the MSDS to identify the product's ingredients (usually listed in Section 3 on the MSDS).
- Avoid using joint compounds that contain crystalline silica or quartz (another common term for crystalline silica).
- Always use dust control methods, regardless of the joint compound's silica content.

Vacuum Dust Collection Systems

Vacuum dust collection (VDC) systems for drywall sanding equipment are commercially available, and studies show that they significantly reduce total dust concentrations. A NIOSH study of the effectiveness of several vacuum dust collection systems showed reductions in total dust exposures ranging from 80 to 97 percent, depending on the system used (NIOSH, 1995).

Similarly, a second study of vacuum systems reported reductions in total dust exposures of 96

percent when used during pole sanding and 95 percent for hand sanding. Both of the resulting exposure levels were well below regulatory limits for total dust (CPWR, 1998).

Figure 1 shows the average reduction in airborne dust measured for four drywall sanding operations—pole-mounted sanding and hand sanding with and without vacuum dust control measures from the CPWR study.[6]

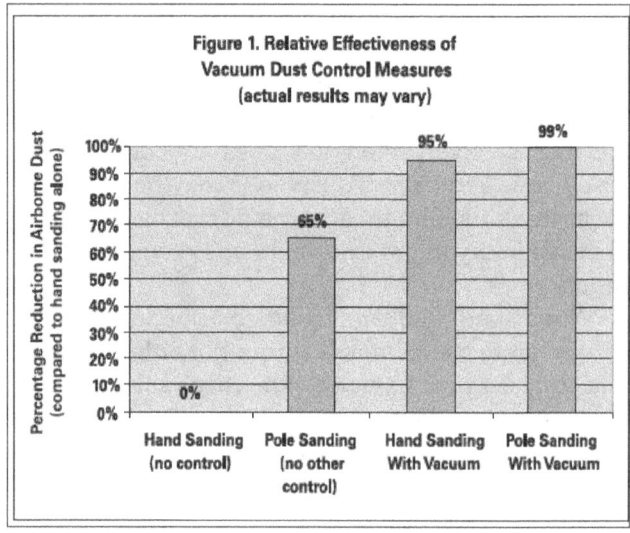

Vacuum dust collection systems typically consist of a sanding screen and a head, with a hose port to connect a portable wet or dry vacuum. Vacuum sanders can be handheld or pole-mounted.

A third study compared the effectiveness of various drywall sanding techniques. The ventilated sander was the most effective in controlling exposures to respirable dust, reducing dust concentrations by 88 percent when compared to a block sander (Young-Corbett and Nussbaum, 2009).

Using and Maintaining the Vacuum

Some dry sanding vacuum system manufacturers recommend using a shop vacuum, while others suggest using industrial vacuums (wet or wet/dry), especially for heavy-duty sanding projects.

Vacuum performance depends largely on how well the filters are maintained. When filters become caked with dust, the vacuum's airflow rate decreases and dust is not captured as efficiently. Some drywall sanding vacuum systems include wet dust collection (air bubbled through water) as a type of prefilter to extend vacuum filter life. Regardless of the type of system used, put the vacuum on a routine maintenance schedule and inspect it frequently.

Tips on Filters

- Use high-efficiency filters for maximum dust control. Typical shop vacuums might not have adequate filtration systems.

- Regularly clean and/or replace filters. Determine the rate at which vacuum filters become clogged or filled and create an appropriate schedule for cleaning and replacing the filters.

- If the vacuum has a "back-pulse" filter cleaning cycle, periodically check this feature to maintain the vacuum's efficiency.

- Take precautions when cleaning or changing vacuum filters, bags and canisters to prevent accidental dust releases.

- Make sure that all vacuum hoses are clean and free of cracks to maintain the correct airflow rate and pressure. Check the entire system daily for signs of poor dust capture or dust leaks and repair accordingly.

- Encourage employees to watch for signs that dust collection equipment is not working efficiently and to make adjustments as necessary.

Vacuum dust collection methods are likely to reduce silica exposures to levels less than 1 mg/m³ while performing drywall finishing. If using a VDC system, the exposure monitoring needs to be performed while it is in operation. This enables you to check the adequacy of the VDC system as well as seeing if it is necessary to use respiratory protection.

Tips for Selecting a Drywall Finishing Tool with Vacuum Dust Collection (NIOSH, 1995)

Most vacuum sanding tools offer dramatic dust reduction. When choosing among tools, employers can concentrate on those features that promote employee acceptance, such as:

- A comfortable handle.
- A lightweight vacuum hose.
- A good connection between the hose and tool.
- Equipment that balances flexibility and stability in the sanding head.
- Models that allow the user to maintain a comfortable posture.

Consider the practical aspects of equipment use. For example:

- For wet collection systems, is it convenient to change the water?
- Will the equipment be easy to clean?
- Will the vacuum be easy to service?

Wet Sponge Method

Wet methods are often the most effective means of controlling dust because particles never have a chance to become airborne. Drywall compound manufacturers often recommend using wet finishing methods for dust control. (NIOSH, 1995). A laboratory study found that use of a wet sponge sanding method reduced respirable dust concentrations by 60 percent when compared to a block sander (Young-Corbett and Nussbaum, 2009).

The wet sanding method for drywall finishing uses a sponge to wet the drywall joint compound and remove residues. For wet sanding, saturate a sponge with clean lukewarm water and wring it out to prevent dripping. Then gently rub the high spots using as few strokes as possible to avoid grooving the joints. The sponge should be cleaned frequently.

In addition to reducing employee exposures, wet finishing methods offer other advantages. For example, wet methods often require less cleanup, the wallboard face is not scuffed during finishing, and joints are easier to conceal with paint than joints that are dry sanded (USG, 2002). Wet finishing can be more complicated on poorly finished joints because employees may find it difficult to remove large amounts of joint compound with this method. Therefore, employees should apply joint compound smoothly so that little finishing is required.

Some contractors are concerned about the increased drying time associated with wet methods. All wet-sanded areas must dry thoroughly before applying additional coats of joint compound or decorating. Some employees, however, already use heat guns or space heaters to shorten joint compound drying times; these methods allow painting to begin sooner, even after wet sanding. Further, the time spent drying the joint compound might be offset by the time it would otherwise take to remove dust particles from the walls before painting.

Tips for Using Drywall Sponges

- Use quality application techniques to minimize excess joint compound on the surface.
- Use as few sanding strokes as possible to avoid grooving the surface.
- Use drying aids to shorten drying time.
- Make sure that sponges and water buckets are thoroughly cleaned after each use to prevent dust from drying on the equipment and becoming airborne.
- Consult manufacturers' recommendations for wet sanding drywall compounds.

Respiratory Protection and Engineering Control Evaluation

Employees who sand drywall without controls are often exposed to high concentrations of dust. This dust may or may not contain respirable silica, depending upon the ingredients in the joint compound. If silica is a component within the joint compound, then it is likely that respirable silica will be released as a particulate. Whether the dust contains silica or not, exposures to drywall sanders are capable of exceeding the PEL for total dust, which is 15 mg/m³, as well as the PEL for respirable dust, which is 5 mg/m³.

The use of silica-free joint compounds, wet methods, and/or effective vacuum dust collection methods are very effective in virtually eliminating or suppressing silica and respirable dust. With the use of such controls, it may be possible to eliminate the need for respiratory protection to control exposures to silica dust.

However, the use of silica-free joint compound alone will not reduce exposures to *respirable dust*. Data suggest that the use of wet methods and vacuum dust collection methods can also reduce respirable dust exposures below 5 mg/m³. With the addition of such controls, respirators may not be needed for protection against respirable dust.

If wet methods or vacuum dust collection methods are not feasible, employees may be required to wear appropriate respiratory protection. A NIOSH approved half-facepiece or disposable respirator with an N-, R- or P-95 filter can protect employees exposed to up to 50 mg/m³ respirable dust.

In any workplace where respirators are necessary to protect the health of the employee, or whenever respirators are required by the employer, the employer must establish and implement a written respiratory protection program with worksite-specific procedures and elements. These sould include the selection of respirators, medical evaluations of employees, fit testing, proper usage, maintenance and care, cleaning and disinfecting, proper air quality/quantity and training (see 29 CFR 1926.103).

Exposure monitoring for respirable dust should be conducted periodically while wet methods or vacuum dust collection methods are being utilized to ensure that engineering controls are working properly and that the proper level of respiratory protection, if necessary, is being used.

For more information on how to determine proper respiratory protection, visit OSHA's Web site at www.osha.gov. NIOSH's Web site also provides information on respirators at www.cdc.gov/niosh.

Compressed Air

The use of compressed air to clean surfaces or clothing is strongly discouraged. Using compressed air to clean work surfaces or clothing can significantly increase employee exposure, especially in enclosed and semi-enclosed spaces. Cleaning should be performed with a HEPA-filtered vacuum or by wet methods.

References

ACGIH. 2001. Threshold limit values for chemical substances and physical agents and biological exposure indices. American Conference of Governmental Industrial Hygienists, Cincinnati, OH.

Center to Protect Workers' Rights (CPWR). 1998. Drywall Dust Engineering Controls. Video VI-98. Produced jointly with National Institute for Occupational Safety and Health (NIOSH) Engineering and Work Practices Controls Work Group.

Epling, C., Gitelman, A., Desai, T. and J. Dement. 1999. Airborne exposures and ambulatory peak expiratory flow in drywall finishers. Report OSH2-98. Center to Protect Workers' Rights.

Lofgren, D.J. 1993. Case studies: Silica exposure for concrete workers and masons. Appl. Occup. Environ. Hyg. 8(10):832-836. October, 1993.

Murray J. and Nadel J., Editors. Textbook of Respiratory Medicine, 2nd Ed., 1994, Airway Pharmacology, pp. 285-311.

NIOSH. 1984. Health Hazard Evaluation Report. Grand Gulf Nuclear Power Plant, Port Gibson, MI. Dept. of Health and Human Services (HETA 83-132-1508). Cincinnati, OH.

NIOSH. 1995. In-depth survey report: a laboratory comparison of conventional drywall sanding techniques versus commercially available control. ECTB 208-11a. National Institute for Occupational Safety and Health.

NIOSH. 1997. Health Hazard Evaluation Report. Center to Protect Workers' Rights. Washington, DC, Dept. of Health and Human Services Report (HETA-94-0078-2660). Cincinnati, OH.

NIOSH 2001. In-depth survey report for four sites: exposure to silica from hand tools in construction chipping, grinding, and hand demolition at Frank Messer and Sons Construction Company, Lexington and Newport, KY, and Columbus and Springfield, OH (EPHB 247-15). National Institute for Occupational Safety and Health, Cincinnati, OH. April, 2001.

NIOSH. 2002. Pocket guide to chemical hazards. Pub. No. 2002-140. National Institute for Occupational Safety and Health, Cincinnati, OH. June, 2002.

OSHA Case Files (Special Emphasis Program Inspection Reports from 1996-1998).

USG. 2002. Finishing and Decorating Gypsum Panels/Wet Sanding. J-610/12-87. http://www.usg.com. (Accessed November 16, 2002.)

Young-Corbett, D.E. and Nussbaum, M.A. (2009). Dust Control Effectiveness of Drywall Sanding Tools. Journal of Occupational and Environmental Hygiene, 6:7, 385-389.

Technical Notes

[1] A 382-minute sample resulted in a respirable dust exposure level of 7.0 mg/m³ and a silica level concentration of 0.21 mg/m³.

[2] Laboratories have not used particle counting for crystalline silica analysis in many years and now report exposure data gravimetrically. However, OSHA's construction PEL for crystalline silica, established in 1971, is still listed as a particle-count value. (See Appendix E to OSHA's National Emphasis Program for Crystalline Silica, CPL 03-00-007, for a detailed discussion of the conversion factor used to transform gravimetric measurements to particle-count values). In this guidance, OSHA is using 0.1 mg/m³ of respirable quartz as an 8-hour time-weighted average as a benchmark to describe the effectiveness of control measures. The benchmark is approximately equivalent to the general industry silica PEL. Other organizations suggest more stringent levels. For example, the National Institute for Occupational Safety and Health (NIOSH) recommends that respirable crystalline silica exposures be limited to 0.05 mg/m³ as a 10-hour time-weighted average (NIOSH, 2002). The American Conference of Governmental Industrial Hygienists (ACGIH) recommends that respirable crystalline silica exposures be limited to 0.025 mg/m³ as an 8-hour time-weighted average (ACGIH, 2008).

[3] Epling (1999) collected 8-hour respirable crystalline silica samples at two construction sites using a 10-millimeter cyclone at 2.6 liters/minute (LPM) airflow to achieve a 4-micrometer cut-point. Crystalline silica was quantifiable at 1.1 to 3.7 percent in four of the six samples. NIOSH (1997) used Dorr-Oliver cyclones at 1.7 LPM to collect 22 samples, of which 15 (68 percent) contained silica amounts between the level of quantification (LOQ) and limit of detection (LOD). In the same report, NIOSH described two additional respirable crystalline silica results from another site as 0.04 and 0.08 mg/m³ for samples of 443 and 435 minutes duration.

[4] These values were those reported in the CPWR video, which may not have shown all measurements taken during the study. Respirable dust levels were not reported (CPWR, 1998).

[5] When the silica percentage is in doubt, some laboratories that specialize in environmental testing can analyze a sample of the product to determine the actual silica content. OSHA recommends, however, that employers minimize employee exposure by relying on manufacturers' information and using dust control methods rather than by testing joint compounds themselves.

[6] Data values were averaged from those presented in the CPWR video, which may not include all values measured during the actual study.

General Housekeeping and Use of Dust Suppressants

This section covers dust control methods for general housekeeping activities at construction sites, including site cleaning, material handling and the use of dust suppressants. The term "silica" used in this document refers to respirable crystalline silica.

Introduction

Exposure to fine particles of silica has been shown to cause silicosis, a serious and sometimes fatal lung disease. Construction employees who inhale fine particles of silica may be at risk of developing this disease. Silica dust can be generated when materials such as ceramics, concrete, masonry, rock and sand are mixed, blasted, chipped, cut, crushed, drilled, dumped, ground, mixed or driven upon. Employees at construction sites may be exposed to silica dust during general housekeeping activities such as sweeping, emptying vacuum cleaners and using compressed air for cleaning. Silica exposures may also occur whenever silica-containing dusts are disturbed, such as during material handling. The small particles generated during these activities easily become suspended in the air and, when inhaled, penetrate deep into employees' lungs.

Examples of Construction Materials that Contain Silica

- Concrete
- Brick, tile and other masonry
- Mortar
- Asphalt
- Sand
- Many stone products (such as granite, slate and sandstone) and rock aggregate[1]

In several studies of construction sites, silica exposure levels rose when employees engaged in general construction cleaning activities such as dry sweeping, using backpack blowing equipment and emptying vacuums used to collect concrete dust.[2] For example, the National Institute for Occupational Safety and Health (NIOSH) determined that a concrete finisher handling a vacuum bag containing concrete dust was exposed to approximately 0.79 mg/m³ (milligrams of silica per cubic meter of air) (NIOSH, 2001b).[3] This level is more than five times higher than the finisher's average silica exposure for

the day, which already exceeded the Occupational Safety and Health Administration's (OSHA) benchmark of 0.1 mg/m³ (milligrams per cubic meter of air) as an 8-hour time-weighted average (TWA), an exposure approximately equivalent to OSHA's general industry permissible exposure limit (PEL).[4] While most employees do not handle vacuum bags for their full shifts, this activity presents a significant source of exposure for employees who may also be exposed to silica from other sources.

Housekeeping Activities that Can Release Airborne Dust Containing Silica

- Dry sweeping
- Using blowers or compressed air for cleaning
- Dumping bags of raw material
- Dumping wheelbarrow loads
- Breaking or crushing materials
- Spreading crushed materials (concrete, aggregate)
- Dropping, tossing, or pouring dusty materials
- Operating a vacuum with the air discharge near a source of dust
- Emptying vacuums
- Driving over piles of dust or debris
- Other actions that disturb or create dust

This section describes several methods available to reduce employees' silica exposure during housekeeping and related activities. These methods include general measures to suppress the creation of dusts (use of water and other dust suppressants), vacuuming, using cabs and enclosures, and modification of work practices. Many of these methods can be used to reduce exposures to silica in a broad range of construction activities in addition to housekeeping tasks.

Visible and Respirable Dust

Visible dust contains large particles that are easy to see. The tiny, respirable-sized particles (those that can get into the deep lung) containing silica pose the greatest hazard and are not visible. Most dust-generating construction activities produce a mixture of visible and respirable particles.

Do use visible dust as a general guide for improving dust suppression efforts. If you see visible dust being generated, emissions of respirable silica are probably too high. Measures that control tool-generated dust at the source usually reduce *all* types of particle emissions, including respirable particles.

Do not rely *only* on visible dust to assess the extent of the silica hazard. There may be more airborne respirable dust present that is not visible to the naked eye.

Silica Dust Control Measures

Dust Suppressants

Dust suppression is a dust control method that can be applied to many different operations, such as materials handling, rock crushing, abrasive blasting and operation of heavy construction vehicles. Types of dust suppressants include water (mists, sprays, steam and fog), surfactants (including foams), acrylic polymers, asphalt, chloride compounds, lignin compounds, natural oil resins, organic resin emulsions and petroleum-based oils and waste products.

Dust suppression is generally effective in controlling respirable silica dust, although few data are available regarding specific exposure reductions. Many of these methods have also been successful in reducing erosion and fugitive dust emissions (PM10) regulated by the Environmental Protection Agency (EPA).[5]

Water

Wet methods (i.e., methods involving the application of water) are often the easiest and most effective way to reduce potential silica exposures. Dust that is wet is less able to become or remain airborne. Water can be applied in different ways to suit the specific situation. For example:

- Wet mopping or spraying water, followed with a wet vacuum or squeegee will collect dust and create less airborne dust than dry sweeping.

- The point where dust will be generated or has settled can be flooded by flushing surfaces with water or wet scrubbing.

- Particles can be removed from surfaces by water under pressure (pressure washing).[6]

Water can be used as a dust suppressant during a variety of activities, including:

- *Use of heavy construction vehicles on unpaved surfaces:* A water truck can spray the site grounds.

- *Blasting operations:* A separate water hose can be strung next to the hose containing the blasting medium; the two materials can be sprayed simultaneously.

- *Materials handling and transport operations:* It is often most efficient to spray a material before it reaches a transfer point so that the dust has time to absorb the water before being disturbed. Increasing moisture content decreases the amount of dust generated (Plinke et al., 1992).

Construction employees can use a variety of equipment to apply water, depending on the size and type of the job. A spray or mist can be an efficient way to distribute adequate amounts of water over a large area. For a small job, a portable garden sprayer with a hand pump may be adequate; a larger job might require a garden hose with a mister nozzle. On a demolition site, a fire hose can be used to apply water rapidly over a large area, but employees must be able to control both the spray nozzle and the water pressure or volume.

Start with a Gentle Spray or Mist

Avoid blasting dry dust with a forceful stream of water. The energy of the water and surrounding air can disturb the dust and cause it to become airborne before it is wet.

Instead, use a gentle spray or mist to moisten the particles first. When washing large quantities of dust from a surface, increase the water force only after pre-wetting all the dust with a gentle spray. Use the minimum amount of water needed to get the job done, particularly where runoff is a concern.

For optimal results:

- Use nozzles and flow regulators to control water volume.

- Clean up water and slurry as soon as practical (using a wet/dry shop vacuum or squeegees and scoops). If allowed to dry, the dust contained in the slurry may become a source of silica and other dust exposure.

- Rewet surfaces as often as necessary to maintain dust control.

Fogging Methods: Fog, fine particles of water, can be an effective dust suppressant in certain situations because it provides a larger contact area than do water sprays. Fog is most effective when the water droplets are approximately the same size in diameter as the dust particles to be suppressed. The dust particles stick to the water droplets. The added weight prevents the particles from remaining suspended in the air.

Water fog can be generated with a two-fluid system that uses water with compressed air to increase impact force on the nozzle impinging device or a single-fluid system where water is pumped at very high pressure and hydraulically forced through a very small nozzle opening.

Fogging works best in a pocket or covered area where air movement is negligible, such as a sealed material transfer point. Because material moistened by fog dries quickly, this method has no lasting benefit and must be repeated at each transfer point of the handling system. Fog is less effective in open areas because the droplets may blow away before contacting the dust. Fog may also reduce visibility and condense on control room windows and may freeze in cold temperatures and evaporate quickly in low-humidity conditions (Westbrook, 1999).

Steam Methods: Steam is the gaseous state of water. Like fog, steam can reach a larger contact area than sprayed water. Also like fog, steam can visually restrict operations and condense on surfaces.

Electrostatic Charging: Particles from most industrial dust clouds possess either a positive or negative charge, (Johnston et al., 1985). For this reason, electrostatically charged water sprays have been studied as a dust suppressant method. Electrostatic water sprays may enhance dust removal by attracting oppositely-charged dust particles to the charged water droplets. An electrostatic water spray emitter consists of a waterproof power supply, a control panel for monitoring and adjusting water and air supply rates, an insulated charging coil and a siphon-type nozzle. Sources of clean air and water are required, with a relatively long period of time to interact (seconds) between the dust particles and water droplets for peak efficiency.

Freezing Temperatures. Freezing temperatures complicate the use of water. Consider heating the local work area, if practical, to prevent ice from forming in the water-feed system. Large portable heating units are commonly used to heat commercial and sometimes road and highway projects. Drain the system when not in use. If water freezes on the ground, chip away the ice or use deicing compounds or sand to control the slipping hazard.

Electrical Safety. Use ground-fault circuit interrupters (GFCIs) and watertight, sealable electrical connectors for electric tools and equipment on construction sites (OSHA, 1996). These features are particularly important to employee safety in wet or damp areas, such as where water is used to control dust. Although an assured equipment grounding conductor program is an acceptable alternative to GFCIs, OSHA recommends that employers use GFCIs where possible because they afford better protection for employees. (See 29 CFR 1926.404(b)(1) for OSHA's ground-fault protection requirements.)

Surfactants and Other Soil-Binding Materials
A surfactant is a highly concentrated soap or detergent that can be added to water to help control dust. Surfactants are often referred to as "wetting agents." Surfactants break the surface tension of water, allowing the water to penetrate deeper, to better saturate the dust particles and slow evaporation. When using surfactants on a ground surface (soil), the surface stays moist longer and fewer water applications are needed.

Surfactants formulated to enhance dust particle water absorption capabilities are not recommended for materials handling system applications because they will make dust particles stick to many other surfaces, such as transfer points and conveyor belts (Westbrook, 1999).

Surfactants formulated to alter the static surface charge of dust particles are generally better for materials handling systems. The surfactant molecules have a high affinity for other surfactants and most other materials, regardless of any static surface charging. This enables the treated dust particles to agglomerate, having higher weight-to-surface area ratios and fewer tendencies to remain or become airborne (Westbrook, 1999).

Surfactants can be applied in either a water or foam spray. Both types rely on the water in the blended solution to act as a carrier by which small quantities of surfactant molecules become applied to the dust particles. Both types reduce fugitive dust amounts by up to 90 percent or more. Water/surfactant sprays generally consist of one part surfactant to 1,000 parts water. (Westbrook, 1999).

In addition to surfactants, a number of other compounds are used on soils to provide dust suppression. These compounds, discussed in greater detail below, include:

- Acrylic polymers;
- Solid asphalt;
- Liquid asphalt;
- Chloride compounds;
- Lignin compounds;
- Natural oil resins; and
- Organic resin emulsions.

Petroleum-based oils and waste products *should not* be used as a dust suppressant as this is a violation of multiple EPA regulations (Skorseth and Selim, 2000).

Acrylic Polymers

Acrylic polymers are synthetic plastic adhesives that work as a ground surface dust suppressant by chemically binding during curing, creating a surface crust. Acrylic polymers may take up to 24 hours to cure, depending on the temperature (colder temperatures result in longer cure times). They are considered environmentally safe, non-corrosive, non-leaching, and non-slippery when wet. Further, they are flexible after curing. Users have found various levels of success with acrylic polymers as a dust suppressant on unpaved roads (Saunders, 2000).

Asphalt - Solids

Asphalt is obtained as a residue in the distillation or refining of petroleum. Recycled asphalt from roads or roofing material can be an economical dust suppression tool on unpaved roadways or when crushing rock. Using millings from asphalt roads as a dust suppressant may have the added benefit of helping county transportation authorities reduce disposal or storage costs for the used material. However, when used on unpaved roadways, millings can contribute to the formation of road ruts, resulting in higher maintenance costs.

Asphalt – Liquids

Liquid asphalts have been used in the past to treat gravel roads for dust control. However, most localities, in compliance with EPA requirements, have banned the use of liquid asphalt products due to the large content of fuel oil or kerosene in these products (Skorseth and Selim, 2000).

Chloride Compounds

Popular in surface dust control and road stabilization, calcium chloride and magnesium chloride are naturally occurring brines processed into a colorless, odorless liquid and into white flakes or pellets. Used as water additives, chloride compounds are hygroscopic and work as dust suppressants by attracting moisture from the air. They resist evaporation. They exhibit high surface tension and low vapor pressure, which helps bind or aggregate smaller particles to larger and heavier particles which are less likely to become airborne.

These properties make chloride compounds effective in keeping unpaved surfaces damp and reducing dust levels. They remain active even after the ground has been tilled or rebladed. Chloride compounds also lower the freezing point of water, making them useful in cold temperatures.

However, these properties also give chloride compounds the disadvantage of performing poorly in low humidity. They can be corrosive without inhibitor additives (though most products contain the necessary inhibitors), may be harmful to vegetation and ground water, and may leach away with precipitation. Further, they may be slippery when wet, so slips and falls may be a concern for employees.

Lignin Compounds

Lignin sulfate and lignin sulfonate are powders that are by-products of the wood pulping process. Compounds in this category chemically bind soil particles together by reducing the tension between clay in the soil and water. They react with negatively-charged clay particles to agglomerate the soil. Lignin compounds are used to coat ground surfaces, forming a crust as they cure.

Lignin compounds are water soluble and are most effective in dry climates. They are immediately active and remain effective after reblading. They lower the freezing point of water, making them useful in cold temperatures.

Lignin sulfates and sulfonates leach away with precipitation and may be slippery when wet. They may also become brittle when dry and can be harmful to ground water. Further, they work best with a well-graded aggregate mix (a wide range in grain sizes). They may have an unpleasant odor when first applied, but the smell dissipates quickly. Lignin compounds may also be corrosive to aluminum.

Natural Oil Resins

Natural oil resins represent another class of dust suppressants. One popular example is soybean oil resin, a by-product of soybean oil refining. Oil resins are usually added to water to make a suspension and applied to ground surfaces. For road stabilization, the oil can be applied in a spray with bituminous asphalt applicator equipment. The oil coating leaves a residue that makes dust particles heavier and makes them stick together like an adhesive, a process known as agglomeration.

Used vegetable oil has also been explored as a dust suppressant (Drenner and Trumbull, 2003). Due to its relatively low cost, it may be an attractive option in some situations, although its performance duration may be limited. (Note that used vegetable oil should not be confused with used motor oil. Used motor oil is restricted or prohibited for use as a dust suppressant in most jurisdictions.)

Vegetable oil has also been used as a dust suppressant in the agriculture industry, specifically to reduce dust in grain storage and processing areas. However, researchers disagree about its effectiveness.

Natural oil products are immediately active, effective after reblading, non-corrosive, and environmentally safe. However, they may have an offensive odor, may become brittle when dry and may leach away with precipitation. They may also be slippery when wet.

Organic Resin Emulsions

Organic resin emulsions are natural resins, emulsified in liquid form such as pine tree sap. They bind and adhere to dust particles as they cure and create a surface crust. They are environmentally safe, non-corrosive, non-leaching, non-slippery when wet, and waterproof. However, they may become brittle when dry and need to be cleaned from equipment quickly. These natural resins will take longer to cure in colder temperatures.

Vacuum Methods

Vacuums offer a versatile option for collecting dry debris from smooth and uneven surfaces, cracks, expansion joints and irregular shapes. Wet/dry vacuums can also collect water, slurry and damp materials. Pneumatic vacuums may be used where electricity is not available.

Vacuums do not produce the clouds of dust often generated during dry sweeping or blowing with compressed air, but they are not dust-free. Vacuum cleaners with inadequate or damaged filters can increase employee silica dust exposures due to the agitating action of the vacuum and incomplete filtration of fine dust particles (Heckel et al., 2000). Employers must choose vacuum filter media carefully.

Understanding vacuum filter ratings. Manufacturers' vacuum filter descriptions can be confusing and make comparison difficult; however, the filter rating system itself is quite simple.

Rating systems indicate a filter's ability to capture various sizes of dust. Two important pieces of information are: (1) collection efficiency, or percent of particles captured, and (2) the smallest size of particles that will be captured at the stated efficiency.

For example, a high efficiency particulate air (HEPA) filter is 99.97 percent efficient against particles as small as 0.3 micrometers (μm). Less-efficient filters report ratings with either lower collection efficiency, larger particle size, or both. Compared to a HEPA filter, a filter rated 70 percent efficient against 7 μm dust, for example, will not capture as many fine particles; the uncaptured particles will be discharged with the vacuum's exhaust air and perhaps into the employees' breathing zone.

Tips for Operating Vacuum Cleaners

- If necessary, train employees on the vacuum's self-cleaning features and the manufacturer's recommended methods for emptying canisters or changing bags.
- Select a vacuum that allows employees to clean filters without opening the vacuum and remove full bags without exposing themselves to dust (NIOSH, 2001b).
- Position vacuums away from sources of dust or first vacuum the area where the canister will sit. If a vacuum sits on a dusty surface, the exhaust air can cause particles to become airborne.
- Keep the vacuum hose clear and free of debris, kinks, and tight bends. Maintain the vacuum at peak performance to ensure adequate airflow through the shroud and ducts.[7]
- On vacuums with reverse flow cleaning systems, activate the system frequently (several times per day, or more if necessary).
- Empty collection bags and vacuums as frequently as necessary to prevent decreased airflow.[8] Follow manufacturers' directions and do not allow units to overfill. Dispose of collected dust in a way that prevents it from becoming resuspended in the air.
- Keep an adequate supply of bags at the worksite.

For greater employee protection, select a vacuum filter that has a higher efficiency against smaller particles.

When purchasing filters (or a new vacuum), keep in mind that the more efficient filters generally also require more "lift" or suction power (measured as "inches of water grade," or "in. w.g."). The higher-efficiency filters are not available for vacuums with low lift ratings.[9]

Higher-efficiency filters tend to be more costly. Extend the service life of more expensive filters by adding prefilters, which protect the fine-particle filter by catching the larger dust. Low-cost prefilters can be changed frequently with minimal expense.

Prefilters are available in various grades. Select a relatively efficient prefilter that will capture most of the dust. An inefficient prefilter will allow more dust to pass, causing the high efficiency particle filter to become overloaded more quickly (Trakumas et al., 2001).

Filter surface area (the size of the filter if it were spread out flat) is another feature to consider when comparing filters. The greater the surface area of the filter, the more dust it will hold. Vacuums also require less suction power to move air through filters with larger areas. Manufacturers often provide information about filter surface area.

Cabs and Enclosures

Use material handling equipment for moving large amounts of silica-containing dusty material. Select equipment with enclosed cabs and positive pressure ventilation systems (to isolate operators from dust) and air conditioning (to encourage operators to keep windows and doors closed, so dust stays out). Many cabs can be retrofitted to add a filtered ventilation system and air conditioning.[10]

Put the cab on a regular maintenance schedule. Check for leaking seals around windows, doors and electrical wiring. Change ventilation system filters on schedule. For maximum protection from exposure to small particles, use the most efficient filter recommended by the cab manufacturer.

Clean the cab interior daily so that dust does not accumulate and is not dispersed by the cab ventilation system.

Compressed Air

The use of compressed air to clean surfaces or clothing is strongly discouraged. Using compressed air to clean work surfaces or clothing can significantly increase employee exposure, especially in enclosed and semi-enclosed spaces. Cleaning should be performed with a HEPA-filtered vacuum or by wet methods.

Work Practices

Common sense work practices can help employees limit their exposure to silica. Examples include:

- Clean up spills and waste before dust can spread.

- Wear a rubber apron to keep wet dust off clothing. When it dries, the dust can become airborne.

- Whenever possible, work upwind of any dust sources. This can be as simple as working from the other side of the pile when shoveling debris.

- Keep roadways damp at sites where the surface includes high silica aggregate or crushed concrete.

- Wet down silica-containing debris and rock spoil piles prior to removal or disturbance.

Encourage employees to watch for dust sources containing silica and make adjustments or use dust control methods to reduce their silica exposure.

Dumping or Pouring Materials

The farther objects fall when dropped, the more dust they will generate on impact. When dumping or pouring materials (for example, debris into a dumpster or raw materials into a mixer), minimize drop distances by releasing materials close to their destination level. Support the bag, bin, or barrow just above the top of the pile and slowly add materials onto the pile. When a long drop is unavoidable, use enclosed disposal chutes or slides.

Use wheelbarrow ramps of appropriate height (not too tall for a small dump pile).

Moisten the dumpster contents, floors and walls prior to adding any debris to reduce dust released upon impact.

Spray the debris stream with water mist to help suppress dust.

Sweeping

Take steps to limit the use of dry sweeping. Reduce the quantity of debris and the distance and frequency of sweeping. Use a vacuum or wet mop, or moisten the material and scrape it into position.

Collect and transport debris by bucket or wheelbarrow from smaller local piles rather than pushing it for longer distances to a central pile.

Avoid dry sweeping debris with sweeping compounds that contain quartz sand (crystalline silica) as the grit.

Removing Debris from Slots or Uneven Surfaces

Use a vacuum instead of a blower. Use vacuum hose attachments sized for the situation. For example, remove tailings from handheld drill holes using a HEPA-filtered vacuum.

Flush cracks with water instead of using compressed air.

Vacuums

Use vacuums with self-cleaning features (back-pulse). Make sure that employees are fully trained in vacuum operation.

Handle vacuum bags carefully and have a disposal receptacle nearby.

Avoid overfilling vacuum canisters or bags. The extra weight makes bags difficult to handle and subject to tearing.

Avoid shaking or jarring the vacuum. Follow the manufacturer's instructions for recommended handling.

Avoid depositing or storing collected debris where it will be disturbed or run over and become a source of dust exposure for another employee.

Case Studies

The following case studies indicate silica exposure levels found under certain uncontrolled or poorly controlled conditions, and show the effectiveness of controls in reducing silica exposures.

Vacuum Bag as Exposure Source

Case Study I: NIOSH evaluated a concrete finisher's silica exposure while he operated a grinder with vacuum dust collection equipment. Investigators determined that a peak period of exposure (0.79 mg/m^3) occurred while the employee was handling the vacuum bag containing concrete dust. This level was more than five times higher than his average silica exposure for the day (0.155 mg/m^3). Because the employee emptied the vacuum frequently (approximately every 35 minutes during a 7-hour shift), the vacuum bag dust probably made a substantial contribution to his total silica exposure for the day (NIOSH, 2001b).

Case Study II. Researchers reported that, at another construction site, a concrete finisher dumped full vacuum bags on the ground, where they became a source of dust exposure when a forklift drove over them and when other employees swept up the spilled dust. The same employee had initially attempted to clean the vacuum filter by removing it and pounding it on the ground. After he received training on the vacuum's self-cleaning feature, he reduced downtime (and probably prolonged the filter's life) by using the vacuum manufacturer's recommended methods (Echt and Sieber, 2002).

Cleanup Activities

Case Study III. In a study of nine construction sites, investigators measured respirable dust and silica exposure of 10 employees performing cleanup activities. During cleaning tasks, the tool associated with the highest dust exposure was the backpack blower (Flanagan et al., 2003).[11]

In the same study, dust exposures were higher for employees who used a sweeping compound than for employees who swept without a compound (Flanagan et al., 2003). The sweeping compound type was not reported, but some compounds include crystalline silica (quartz sand) as grit, which

might be an additional source of silica dust during sweeping (NIOSH, 2001a).

Using Box Fans

This study also found that dust exposure levels were higher for employees performing cleanup activities in areas where box fans were used, compared to cleanup in areas without fans (Flanagan et al., 2003). Air blowing on sources of dust can increase the amount of dust in the air.

Although the investigators report an *average* employee exposure level of 0.03 mg/m^3 (below OSHA's limits) for employees performing cleanup, half of the employees' exposure levels exceeded 0.05 mg/m^3 (Flanagan et al., 2003).[12]

Dry Sweeping

Case Study IV. A study conducted at nine construction sites in Finland evaluated the relative average respirable crystalline silica exposure levels for employees' dry sweeping after various stages of demolition and construction, and compared them with exposures when alternate cleaning methods were used. Compared to dry sweeping, employee exposures were approximately 50 percent lower when the employees used squeegees to sweep (scrape) surfaces and approximately 80 percent lower when employees used vacuums (Riala, 1988).[13]

Using Steam

Case Study V. Testing was performed at two mineral processing plants to determine the effectiveness of steam as a dust suppressant. Applying water vapor as steam (0.22 percent water-to-product ratio by weight) resulted in a 64 percent reduction in respirable dust. This compares to a reduction in respirable dust of 25 percent when the same amount of water was applied as a water spray. Even when the amount of water sprayed was increased to 0.5 percent (water-to-product ratio by weight), the reduction in respirable dust (55 percent) was less than that achieved with steam (Bureau of Mines, 1985).

Comparison Study I

A university study compared various types of dust suppressants for use on unpaved roadways: asphalt millings, calcium chloride, magnesium chloride, lignosulfonate (tree sap), soybean oil, and used fryer oil. The researchers developed a scoring system that took into account environmental impact and dust suppression performance. Lignosulfonate achieved the highest score. However, the authors noted that a second application of the product was needed. The two oil compounds scored evenly, just below lignosulfonate, but the authors noted that the vegetable oils required more intensive maintenance than other dust suppressants. The roadway treated with used fryer oil became rutted early in the study. The two chloride compounds achieved scores slightly less than the oils. All options significantly outscored the untreated (control) section of roadway (Drenner and Trumbull, 2003).

Comparison Study II

Another university study compared the cost and performance of three dust suppression and soil stabilization options (lignosulfonate, calcium chloride, magnesium chloride), and the impact of no treatment on an unpaved roadway over 4½ months. The dust suppressants reduced fugitive dust emissions by 50 to 70 percent compared to the untreated section. The researchers estimated that the untreated test section of roadway would require maintenance eight times per year versus twice a year for the treated sections. The researchers noted pothole formation on the lignosulfonate-treated section of roadway after the test period ended. When material, labor, equipment and maintenance costs were tallied, researchers estimated an annual cost of more than $20,000 per mile for an untreated roadway. Calcium chloride, lignosulfonate, and magnesium chloride treatments were estimated to have approximate annual costs of $11,000, $10,000, and $9,000 dollars per mile, respectively (Addo and Sanders, 1995).

Comparison Study III

NIOSH evaluated substitute materials for silica sand in abrasive blasting. Among the many products compared to silica sand was silica sand treated with three different types of dust suppressants. Although the report did not reveal the names and types of dust suppressants, airborne testing revealed that dust suppressants reduced respirable silica levels by 70 percent compared to untreated silica sand (NIOSH, 1998).

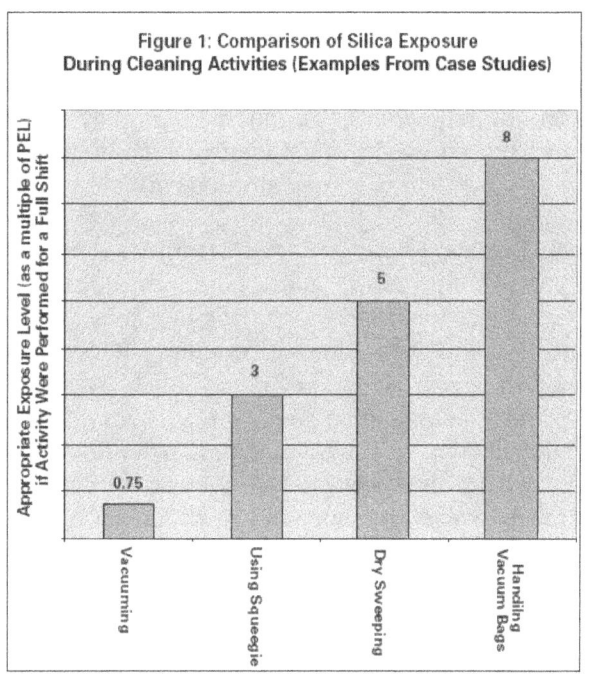

Figure 1: Comparison of Silica Exposure During Cleaning Activities (Examples From Case Studies)

Respiratory Protection and Engineering Control Evaluation

Tasks performed during general housekeeping, such as dry sweeping, dumping materials, emptying vacuum cleaners and using compressed air, can contribute significantly to employees' exposure to respirable silica. Control methods including use of dust suppressants, vacuuming, use of cabs and enclosures, and modification of work practices can be applied to reduce silica exposure while performing general housekeeping tasks. Utilizing these methods in the manner that has been presented in this section will, in most if not all cases, allow employees who are performing general housekeeping to perform the operation without respiratory protection.

Where engineering and work practice controls are not sufficient to reduce employees' exposure below 0.1 mg/m³, respiratory protection may be needed (see 29 CFR 1926.103). If respiratory protection is necessary, use a properly-fitted, NIOSH-approved half-facepiece or disposable respirator equipped with an N-, R- or P-95 filter. In the occasional situation where general housekeeping tasks are performed for a full 8-hour day, time-weighted average silica exposures may exceed 1.0 mg/m³. In these situations, a full facepiece respirator, which provides greater protection than a half-facepiece respirator, may be necessary.

In any workplace where respirators are necessary to protect the health of the employee, or whenever respirators are required by the employer, the employer must establish and implement a written respiratory protection program with worksite-specific procedures and elements, including the selection of respirators, medical evaluations of employees, fit testing, proper usage, maintenance and care, cleaning and disinfecting, proper air quality/quantity and training (see 29 CFR 1926.103).

Uncontrolled housekeeping activities, such as the use of compressed air, can contribute substantial excess exposure to nearby employees within a short period of time. Alternate methods of cleaning should be explored.

Employers should conduct exposure monitoring periodically while controls are being used to ensure that the controls are working properly and that the appropriate level of respiratory protection is being used.

For more information on how to determine proper respiratory protection, visit OSHA's Web site at www.osha.gov. NIOSH's Web site also provides information on respirators at www.cdc.gov/niosh.

References

ACGIH. 2001. Industrial Ventilation, a Manual of Recommended Practice, 25th edition. American Conference of Governmental Industrial Hygienists, Cincinnati, OH.

ACGIH. 2008. Threshold limit values for chemical substances and physical agents and biological exposure indices. American Conference of Governmental Industrial Hygienists, Cincinnati, OH.

Addo, J.Q. and Sanders, T.J. 1995. Effectiveness and environmental impact of road dust suppressants. Mountain-Plains Consortium Report No. 95-28A.

Beardwood, J. 2001. Dust gets in your eyes...lungs, wallet, and other wear parts. Grading and Excavation Contractor. www.forester.net/gx_0106_dust.html.

Bureau of Mines. 1985. Adding steam to control dust in mineral processing. Report of Investigation No. 8935, 1985.

Drenner, J., and T. Trumbull. 2003. Preliminary report on used fryer oil as a dust suppressant. P² Highlight. (January) www.iwrc/org/p2highlt/p2current.cfm.

Echt, A., and W.K. Sieber. 2002. Case Studies: Control of silica exposure from hand tools in construction: Grinding concrete. Appl. Occup. Environ. Hygiene. 17(7):457-461. July, 2002.

Flanagan, M.E., N. Seixas, M. Majar, J. Camp, and M. Morgan. 2003. Silica dust exposures during selected construction activities. Am. Ind. Hygiene Assn. J 64(3):319-28. May-June, 2003.

Grenier, M.G. and Bigu, J.. 1988. Suppression of airborne dust in hard rock mines by means of electrostatic water sprays. Appl. Ind. Hygiene. 3:251-257. September, 1988.

Heckel, C.L., A. Quraishi, N.G. Carlson, and A.J. Streifel. 2000. Evaluation of vacuum cleaners: A method to evaluate the cleaning effectiveness and airborne particle generation of vacuum cleaners. Poster presented at 2000 American Industrial Hygiene Conference and Exposition.

Hogan, T.J. 1996. Selected particulates: silica. In Plog, B.A., J. Niland, and P.J. Quinlan, eds. Fundamentals of Industrial Hygiene, 4th ed. National Safety Council. Itasca, IL, pp. 180-182, 1996.

Johnston, A.M., J.H. Vincent, and A.D. Jones. 1985. Measurement of electric charge for workplace aerosols. Ann. Occup. Hygiene. 29:2, 1985.

McKernan, J. 2000. Personal communication between J. McKernan of National Institute for Occupational Safety and Health and L. Lewis of Eastern Research Group, January 28, 2000.

NIOSH. 1998. Evaluation of substitute materials for silica sand in abrasive blasting. Report prepared under contract 200-95-2946. National Institute for Occupational Safety and Health. Pittsburgh, PA. September, 1998.

NIOSH. 1999a. Control technology and exposure assessment for occupational exposure to crystalline silica: case 04 -- a concrete finishing operation. Report # ECTB 233-104c. National Institute for Occupational Safety and Health, Cincinnati, OH. April, 1999.

NIOSH. 1999b. Control technology and exposure assessment for occupational exposure to crystalline silica: case 15 -- concrete cutting. Report # ECTB 233-115c. National Institute for Occupational Safety and Health, Cincinnati, OH. November, 1999.

NIOSH. 2000. In-depth survey report: Control technology for environmental enclosures -- an evaluation of in-use enclosures at San Joaquin Helicopter. National Institute for Occupational Safety and Health, Cincinnati, OH, 1999.

NIOSH. 2001a. Technology news: Sweeping compound application reduces dust from soiled floors within enclosed operator cabs (No. 487). National Institute for Occupational Safety and Health, Pittsburgh, PA. March, 2001.

NIOSH. 2001b. In-depth survey report of exposure to silica from hand tools in construction chipping, grinding, and hand demolition at Frank Messer and Sons Construction Company: Lexington and Newport, KY, Columbus and Springfield, OH. Report # 247-15. National Institute for Occupational Safety and Health, Cincinnati, OH, April, 2001.

NIOSH. 2002a. In-depth survey report of exposure to silica from demolition of plaster ceilings at Frank Messer and Sons Construction Company: Columbus, OH. Report # 247-15b. National Institute for Occupational Safety and Health, Cincinnati, OH, January, 2002.

NIOSH. 2002b. Pocket guide to chemical hazards. Pub. No. 2002-140. National Institute for Occupational Safety and Health, Cincinnati, OH. June, 2002.

OSHA Case Files (Special Emphasis Program Inspection Reports from 1996-1998).

Plinke, M.A.E., Maus, R. and Leith, D. 1992. Experimental examination of factors that affect dust generation by using Heubach and MRI testers. Am. Ind. Hygiene. Assn. J. 53(5):325-330. May, 1992.

Riala, R. 1988. Dust and quartz exposure of Finnish construction site cleaners. Ann. Occup. Hygiene 32(2):215-220, 1988.

Saunders, Mark. 2000. Just say 'No' to dust…maybe. Grading and Excavation Contractor. May/June. www.forester.net/gec_0005_just.html.

Skorseth, K. and Selim, A.. 2000. Gravel Roads Maintenance and Design Manual. USDOT, Federal Highway Administration. November, 2000.

Smandych, R.S., Thomson, M. and Goodfellow, H. 1998. Dust control for material handling operations: a systematic approach. Am. Ind. Hygiene Assn. J. 58:139-146. February, 1998.

Trakumas, S., Willeke, K., Ginshpun, S.A., Reponen, T., Mainelis, G. and Freidman, W. 2001. Particle emission characteristics of filter-equipped vacuum cleaners. Am. Ind. Hygiene Assn. J. 62:482-493. July/August, 2001.

Westbrook, T. 1999. Managing fugitive dust. Presentation made at the Pollution Prevention Seminar for the Mining and Mineral Industries, Options for Reducing Dust Emissions, held in Mesa, AZ, on September 16, 1999.

Technical Notes

[1] Aggregates can contain up to 80 percent crystalline silica (Hogan, 1996). On the other hand, limestone and marble contain relatively little crystalline silica, often less than 3 percent.

[2] References: Flanagan et al., 2003; NIOSH, 2002a, 1999a, 1999b; OSHA Case Files; Riala, 1988.

[3] NIOSH conducted video and real-time respirable dust monitoring in the employee's breathing zone and simultaneously captured respirable dust on a cassette for gravimetric and X-ray diffraction analysis. Results indicated the respirable dust on the filter was 14.5 percent silica. This percentage was used to calculate the approximate silica exposure associated with the videotaped activities. NIOSH also sampled the employee's full shift using traditional methods. Results indicated an 8-hour time-weighted average respirable silica exposure of 0.155 mg/m^3 (0.182 mg/m^3 for the 410-minute period sampled) (NIOSH, 2001b).

[4] Laboratories have not used particle counting for crystalline silica analysis for many years. Exposure data is now reported gravimetrically. However, OSHA's construction PEL for crystalline silica, established in 1971, is still listed as a particle-count value. (See Appendix E to OSHA's National Emphasis Program for Crystalline Silica, CPL 03-00-007, for a detailed discussion of the conversion factor used to transform gravimetric measurements to particle-count values). In this guidance, OSHA is using 0.1 mg/m^3 of respirable quartz as an 8-hour time-weighted average as a benchmark to describe the effectiveness of control measures. The benchmark is approximately equivalent to the general industry silica PEL. Other organizations suggest more stringent levels. For example, the National Institute for Occupational Safety and Health (NIOSH) recommends that respirable crystalline silica exposures be limited to 0.05 mg/m^3 as a 10-hour time-weighted average (NIOSH, 2002b). The American Conference of Governmental Industrial Hygienists (ACGIH) recommends that respirable crystalline silica exposures be limited to 0.025 mg/m^3 as an 8-hour time-weighted average (ACGIH, 2008).

[5] PM10 is EPA's designation for suspended particulate matter with a mass median aerodynamic diameter less than 10 micrometers (a particle size comparable to that of respirable dust). The amount of this particulate matter is regulated in the National Ambient Air Quality Standards, with the limits being no more than 150 micrograms per cubic meter of air (μg/m^3) in a 24-hour period more than three times in three years, and with an annual arithmetic average not to exceed 50 μg/m^3.

[6] For better dust management, moisten loose dust with a gentle spray before using higher pressure.

[7] ACGIH recommends 3,500 to 4,000 feet per minute (FPM) velocity (within the hose/duct) to keep concrete dust and particles released from grinding from settling in the hose (ACGIH, 2001). For a typical 2-

inch diameter vacuum hose, 75 to 90 cubic feet per minute (CFM) will achieve that duct velocity (ACGIH, 2001). However, for maximum collection efficiency, the shroud may require higher CFM.

[8] NIOSH (2001b) showed that airflow through a vacuum dropped by two-thirds (from 87 to 31 CFM) as the vacuum bag filled. The lower airflow was not adequate to prevent dust from settling in the hose.

[9] For some small vacuums, "pleated" filters with large surface areas can help solve the problem of low suction power.

[10] Controlled tests of aerosol penetration into agricultural tractor cabs have shown that a retrofitted cabin can filter out 99.6 percent of particles 0.3 μm to 0.4 μm in diameter (NIOSH, 2000).

[11] Flanagan et al., 2003, evaluated peak and average respirable dust exposure using personal dust monitors to record multiple one-minute average results during various phases of a task. Observers recorded work variables for each minute.

[12] Eleven crystalline silica samples associated with employees performing cleanup were collected using nylon cyclones and air sampling pumps. Results were reported by major activity group (cleanup) as geometric mean and as percent exceeding the ACGIH TLV (0.05 mg/m³). Employees recorded their own activities during the period sampled (sample durations were not reported, but were less than full-shift) (Flanagan et al., 2003).

[13] Riala (1988) analyzed respirable quartz using sedimentation to separate particles less than 5 μm from total dust samples, rather than by sampling with a cyclone. Additionally, respirable quartz was analyzed in 9 of 110 samples and estimated for the remainder. The average breathing zone silica results were 0.530 mg/m³ for dry sweeping, 0.33 mg/m³ when squeegees were used, and 0.06 to 0.10 mg/m³ during vacuum cleaning. Mean sample durations were approximately 90 minutes. Cleanup worker exposures were notably higher than reported by Flanagan et al., 2003.

OSHA Assistance

OSHA can provide extensive help through a variety of programs, including technical assistance about effective safety and health programs, state plans, workplace consultations, voluntary protection programs, strategic partnerships, and training and education.

Safety and Health Program Management System Guidelines

Effective management of employee safety and health protection is a decisive factor in reducing the extent and severity of work-related injuries and illnesses and their related costs. In fact, an effective safety and health management system forms the basis of good employee protection, can save time and money, increase productivity and reduce employee injuries, illnesses and related workers' compensation costs.

To assist employers and employees in developing effective safety and health management systems, OSHA published recommended Safety and Health Program Management Guidelines (54 Federal Register (16): 3904-3916, January 26, 1989). These voluntary guidelines can be applied to all places of employment covered by OSHA.

The guidelines identify four general elements critical to the development of a successful safety and health management system:
- Management leadership and employee involvement,
- Worksite analysis,
- Hazard prevention and control, and
- Safety and health training.

The guidelines recommend specific actions, under each of these general elements, to achieve an effective safety and health management system. The *Federal Register* notice is available online at www.osha.gov.

State Programs

The *Occupational Safety and Health Act of 1970* (OSH Act) encourages states to develop and operate their own job safety and health plans. OSHA approves and monitors these plans. Twenty-four states, Puerto Rico and the Virgin Islands currently operate approved state plans: 22 cover both private and public (state and local government) employment; Connecticut, New Jersey, New York and the Virgin Islands cover the public sector only. States and territories with their own OSHA-approved occupational safety and health plans must adopt standards identical to, or at least as effective as, the Federal OSHA standards.

Consultation Services

Consultation assistance is available on request to employers who want help in establishing and maintaining a safe and healthful workplace. Largely funded by OSHA, the service is provided at no cost to the employer. Primarily developed for smaller employers with more hazardous operations, the consultation service is delivered by state governments employing professional safety and health consultants. Comprehensive assistance includes an appraisal of all mechanical systems, work practices, and occupational safety and health hazards of the workplace and all aspects of the employer's present job safety and health program. In addition, the service offers assistance to employers in developing and implementing an effective safety and health program. No penalties are proposed or citations issued for hazards identified by the consultant. OSHA provides consultation assistance to the employer with the assurance that his or her name and firm and any information about the workplace will not be routinely reported to OSHA enforcement staff.

Under the consultation program, certain exemplary employers may request participation in OSHA's Safety and Health Achievement Recognition Program (SHARP). Eligibility for participation in SHARP includes receiving a comprehensive consultation visit, demonstrating exemplary achievements in workplace safety and health by abating all identified hazards, and developing an excellent safety and health program.

Employers accepted into SHARP may receive an exemption from programmed inspections (not complaint or accident investigation inspections) for a period of 1 year. For more information concerning consultation assistance, see OSHA's website at www.osha.gov.

Voluntary Protection Programs (VPP)

Voluntary Protection Programs and on-site consultation services, when coupled with an effective enforcement program, expand employee protection to help meet the goals of the OSH Act. The VPPs motivate others to achieve excellent safety and health results in the same outstanding way as they establish a cooperative relationship between employers, employees, and OSHA.

For additional information on VPP and how to apply, contact the OSHA regional offices listed at the end of this publication.

Strategic Partnership Program

OSHA's Strategic Partnership Program, the newest member of OSHA's cooperative programs, helps encourage, assist, and recognize the efforts of partners to eliminate serious workplace hazards and achieve a high level of employee safety and health. Whereas OSHA's Consultation Program and VPP entail one-on-one relationships between OSHA and individual worksites, most strategic partnerships seek to have a broader impact by building cooperative relationships with groups of employers and employees. These partnerships are voluntary, cooperative relationships between OSHA, employers, employee representatives, and others (e.g., trade unions, trade and professional associations, universities, and other government agencies).

For more information on this and other cooperative programs, contact your nearest OSHA office, or visit OSHA's website at www.osha.gov.

Alliance Program

Through the Alliance Program, OSHA works with groups committed to safety and health, including businesses, trade or professional organizations, unions and educational institutions, to leverage resources and expertise to develop compliance assistance tools and resources and share information with employers and employees to help prevent injuries, illnesses and fatalities in the workplace.

Alliance program agreements have been established with a wide variety of industries including meat, apparel, poultry, steel, plastics, maritime, printing, chemical, construction, paper and telecommunications. These agreements are addressing many safety and health hazards and at-risk audiences, including silica, fall protection, amputations, immigrant workers, youth and small businesses. By meeting the goals of the Alliance Program agreements (training and education, outreach and communication, and promoting the national dialogue on workplace safety and health), OSHA and the Alliance Program participants are developing and disseminating compliance assistance information and resources for employers and employees such as electronic assistance tools, fact sheets, toolbox talks, and training programs.

OSHA Training and Education

OSHA area offices offer a variety of information services, such as compliance assistance, technical advice, publications, audiovisual aids and speakers for special engagements. OSHA's Training Institute in Arlington Heights, IL, provides basic and advanced courses in safety and health for Federal and state compliance officers, state consultants, Federal agency personnel, and private sector employers, employees, and their representatives.

The OSHA Training Institute also has established OSHA Training Institute Education Centers to address the increased demand for its courses from the private sector and from other federal agencies. These centers are colleges, universities, and nonprofit organizations that have been selected after a competition for participation in the program.

OSHA also provides funds to nonprofit organizations, through grants, to conduct workplace training and education in subjects where OSHA believes there is a lack of workplace training. Grants are awarded annually. Grant recipients are expected to contribute 20 percent of the total grant cost.

For more information on grants, training, and education, contact the OSHA Training Institute, Directorate of Training and Education, 2020 South Arlington Heights Road, Arlington Heights, IL 60005, (847) 297-4810, or see *Training* on OSHA's website at www.osha.gov. For further information on any OSHA program, contact your nearest OSHA regional office listed at the end of this publication.

Information Available Electronically

OSHA has a variety of materials and tools available on its website at www.osha.gov. These include electronic compliance assistance tools, such as *Safety and Health Topics, eTools, Expert Advisors;* regulations, directives and publications; videos and other information for employers and employees. OSHA's software programs and compliance assistance tools walk you through challenging safety and health issues and common problems to find the best solutions for your workplace.

A wide variety of OSHA materials, including standards, interpretations, directives and more can be purchased on CD-ROM from the U.S. Government Printing Office, Superintendent of Documents, toll-free phone (866) 512-1800.

OSHA Publications

OSHA has an extensive publications program. For a listing of free items, visit OSHA's website at www.osha.gov or contact the OSHA Publications Office, U.S. Department of Labor, 200 Constitution Avenue, NW, N-3101, Washington, DC 20210; telephone (202) 693-1888 or fax to (202) 693-2498.

Contacting OSHA

To report an emergency, file a complaint, or seek OSHA advice, assistance, or products, call (800) 321-OSHA or contact your nearest OSHA Regional or Area office listed at the end of this publication. The teletypewriter (TTY) number is (877) 889-5627.

Written correspondence can be mailed to the nearest OSHA Regional or Area Office listed at the end of this publication or to OSHA's national office at: U.S. Department of Labor, Occupational Safety and Health Administration, 200 Constitution Avenue, N.W., Washington, DC 20210.

By visiting OSHA's website at www.osha.gov, you can also:
* File a complaint online,
* Submit general inquiries about workplace safety and health electronically, and
* Find more information about OSHA and occupational safety and health.

OSHA Regional Offices

Region I
(CT,* ME, MA, NH, RI, VT*)
JFK Federal Building, Room E340
Boston, MA 02203
(617) 565-9860

Region II
(NJ,* NY,* PR,* VI*)
201 Varick Street, Room 670
New York, NY 10014
(212) 337-2378

Region III
(DE, DC, MD,* PA, VA,* WV)
The Curtis Center
170 S. Independence Mall West
Suite 740 West
Philadelphia, PA 19106-3309
(215) 861-4900

Region IV
(AL, FL, GA, KY,* MS, NC,* SC,* TN*)
61 Forsyth Street, SW, Room 6T50
Atlanta, GA 30303
(404) 562-2300

Region V
(IL, IN,* MI,* MN,* OH, WI)
230 South Dearborn Street
Room 3244
Chicago, IL 60604
(312) 353-2220

Region VI
(AR, LA, NM,* OK, TX)
525 Griffin Street, Room 602
Dallas, TX 75202
(972) 850-4145

Region VII
(IA,* KS, MO, NE)
Two Pershing Square
2300 Main Street, Suite 1010
Kansas City, MO 64108-2416
(816) 283-8745

Region VIII
(CO, MT, ND, SD, UT,* WY*)
1999 Broadway, Suite 1690
PO Box 46550
Denver, CO 80202-5716
(720) 264-6550

Region IX
(AZ,* CA,* HI,* NV,* and American Samoa,
Guam and the Northern Mariana Islands)
90 7th Street, Suite 18-100
San Francisco, CA 94103
(415) 625-2547

Region X
(AK,* ID, OR,* WA*)
1111 Third Avenue, Suite 715
Seattle, WA 98101-3212
(206) 553-5930

   * These states and territories operate their own OSHA-approved job safety and health programs and cover state and local government employees as well as private sector employees. The Connecticut, New Jersey, New York and Virgin Islands plans cover public employees only. States with approved programs must have standards that are identical to, or at least as effective as, the Federal OSHA standards.

   Note: To get contact information for OSHA Area Offices, OSHA-approved State Plans and OSHA Consultation Projects, please visit us online at www.osha.gov or call us at 1-800-321-OSHA.

www.ingramcontent.com/pod-product-compliance
Lightning Source LLC
Chambersburg PA
CBHW081605170526
45166CB00009B/2840